Sanjeev Kapoor

Mithai

Popular
prakashan

www.popularprakashan.com

Sanjeev Kapoor

Mithai

Sweets for every celebration

In association with Alyona Kapoor

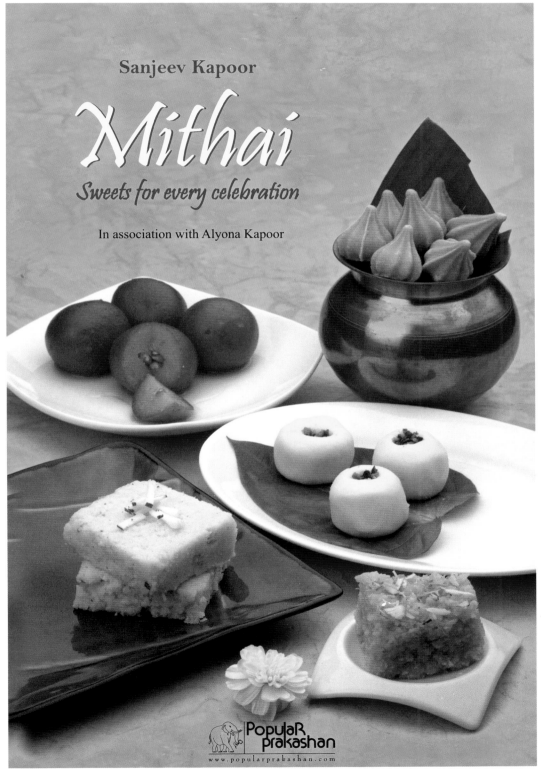

Popular
Prakashan
www.popularprakashan.com

Published by
POPULAR PRAKASHAN PVT. LTD.
301, Mahalaxmi Chambers
22, Bhulabhai Desai Road
Mumbai – 400 026
for KHANA KHAZANA PUBLICATIONS PVT. LTD.

(4415)
ISBN: 978-81-7991-667-4

Design: Anjali Sawant & Mahendra Ghanekar
Food Styling: Anupa Das
Photography: Vikas Shinde

Printed in India
by Nutech Photolithographers
B-240, Okhla Ind. Area, Phase I
New Delhi - 110020

AUTHOR'S NOTE

I have been receiving many requests for a book on mithai from food lovers who want to try their hand at churning out the sweet delicacies at home. From the vast variety of mithai commercially available, I have chosen a few that can easily be prepared at home.

India, with its many regions and cultures is the home to a mind-boggling variety of mithai made from fruit, vegetables, grains, legumes, milk and milk products, all sweetened with sugar or jaggery and enriched with ghee. Every region has its speciality. While in Eastern India, chhena forms the mainstay of mithai (Rosogulla, Sandesh, Rajbhog.), in North India, mawa or khoya is more popular (as in Mathura ka Peda, Mawa Gujiya, Mawa Burfi). In the Western and Southern regions, pulses and legumes are used to advantage (Mohanthaal, Ukdiche Modak, Mysore Paak, Raghavdas Laadoo etc.).

Whatever the region, every happy occasion, festival or celebration is incomplete without something sweet. Mithai are also offered as good luck charms before important events such as interviews and examinations: think dahi aur shakkar to bring good luck and success!

Rich as they may be in calories, sweets when made at home can be made healthier, by controlling the sugar and the fat to a certain extent. I have also included a few recipes, which have been made suitable for those who have to abstain from sugar. You can now treat yourself to Besan ke Laddoo, Kesar-Pista Phirni, Mawa Gujiya or Khajur aur Akhrot ka Roll without worrying about their effect on your weight or blood sugar levels. Having said that, I would repeat the mantra: everything in moderation is good and excess is bad. So enjoy these sweets but do not forget your exercise regime. Good health after all is sweeter than any sweet!

Happy Cooking!

Sanjeev Kapoor

CONTENTS

BEFORE YOU BEGIN

BURFI, PEDA & KHOYA MITHAI

Coconut Burfi 10
Banana Halwa Burfi 12
Besan Burfi 13
Gajar Halwa Burfi 14
Kaju-Kesar Burfi 16
Chocolate Burfi 17
Sev Burfi 18
Mawa Burfi 20
Til Burfi 20
Kesar Burfi 21
Malai Peda 22
Chocolate Peda 24
Kesari Peda 25
Mathura ka Peda 26
Gulab Jamun 28
Mawa-Anjeer Burfi 29
Stuffed Gulab Jamun 30
Mawa Modak 32
Kala Jamun 33

LADDOO, KATLI & ROLLS

Raghavdas Laadoo 36
Churma Laddoo 38
Kurmura Laddoo 39
Kaju, Khoya aur Besan ke Laddoo 40
Motichoor Laddoo 42
Choco-Coconut Laddoo 43
Tilache Laddoo 44
Badam Katli 46
Pista Katli 47
Kaju-Pista-Badam-Kesar Burfi 48
Pista Roll 50
Kaju-Pista Roll 51

CHHENA & PANEER MITHAI

Chum Chum 54
Rosogulla 56
Chhena Murki 57
Sandesh 58
Kheer Kadam 59
Raj Bhog 60
Malai Sandwich 62
Kesari Indrayani 63
Rasmalai 64

SUGAR-FREE MITHAI

Mawa Gujiya	68
Khajur aur Akhrot ka Roll	70
Khajurachi Wadi	71
Steamed Sandesh	72
Besan ke Laddoo	72
Kesar-Pista Phirni	73
Kesari Shrikhand	74
Mango Burfi	75

MITHAI PLATTER

Lavang Latika	78
Dhoda	80
Angoori Petha	81
Milk Powder Gulab Jamun	82
Chandrakala	82
Chocolate-Walnut Fudge	84
Balushahi	85
Ghevar	86
Bombay Halwa	88
Guava Cheese	89
Jalebi	90
Gur Pare	91
Gurpapdi	92

Parwal ki Mithai	92
Ukdiche Modak	94
Kunda	96
Kalakand	97
Malpua	98
Milk Cake	99
Imarti	100
Pinni	101
Mohanthaal	102
Mysore Paak	103

GLOSSARY	104

BEFORE YOU BEGIN...

SOME TERMS AND INGREDIENTS EXPLAINED

ALUM

Alum is a chemical compound – a double sulfate of ammonium – which is used in a range of industrial and culinary processes. It is soluble in water and has an astringent, acid, and sweetish taste. When heated it liquefies. It is used for making certain desserts like Kalakand. When added to milk, it turns granular without splitting completely.

CHHENA

Cow's milk is used to make *chhena* as it has a low fat content. To make *chhena*, bring the milk to a boil in a pan;, reduce the heat and add vinegar. Stir till the milk curdles completely and the solids separate from the whey. Strain and transfer the *chhena* to a piece of muslin to make a *potli*. Drain well. The whey can be used to curdle more milk subsequently. Use 1 tablespoon of vinegar for for every litre of milk. The shelf life of cottage cheese is short, as it is prepared from fresh milk, consume the sweets made from *chhena* as soon as possible.

CITRIC ACID

Citric acid or *nimbu ka phool* is a weak organic acid, which is a natural preservative. It is also used to add an acidic, or sour, taste to foods and soft drinks. It is available as white crystals. It can also be added to caramels to prevent crystallization and to curdle milk when making *peda*.

GUM RESIN

Gum resin (*gond* or *gaund*) is a tree resin that is edible. It is usually sold as small yellowish crystals. The crystals should be fried till swollen and then added to the *mithai*.

KHOYA

• *Khoya* or *mawa* is a form of dried or semi-solid milk, made by boiling milk and reducing it to the desired consistency. It forms the base for a variety of *mithai*. As *khoya* is prepared from fresh milk, *mithai* made with *khoya* has a short shelf life of two to four days if stored in a refrigerator.

• *Hariyali khoya/chikna khoya* is made from cow's milk which is lower in fat content as compared to buffalo milk. It is slightly yellowish in colour and has a loose, sticky consistency. It has a higher moisture content than the regular *khoya* and is used to make *gulab jamun*.

6

SUGAR SYRUP

To make a smooth sugar syrup

Bring the sugar and water to a boil in a non-stick pan over medium heat, stirring continuously. To prevent crystallisation, completely dissolve the sugar before the mixture boils. Brush down any sugar grains that stick to the side of the pan with a clean pastry brush dipped in water. Adding liquid glucose to sugar syrup also helps in preventing crystals from forming.

To clarify a sugar syrup

Boil sugar and water together in a pan. When the sugar dissolves, add a few tablespoons of milk. As the syrup boils the scum will rise to the top. Remove it carefully either with a strainer or with a ladle and discard.

To measure the consistency of sugar syrup

- One string consistency: When a small quantity tested between thumb and forefinger, a long string is formed.
- Two string consistency: When tested between thumb and forefinger, two strings are formed .
- Soft ball consistency: When a few drops of the syrup are put in cold water, you can roll them with your fingers into a soft ball.
- Hard ball consistency: When a few drops of the syrup are put in cold water, you can roll them up with your fingers into a slightly hard ball.

You can also measure the consistency of sugar syrup with a candy thermometer.

TO COAT THE BACK OF A SPOON

This is a cooking technique used to test if a liquid mixture (usually a custard or sauce) is cooked to the right consistency. Dip a wooden or metal spoon into the mixture, remove and run your finger down the back of the spoon. If the mixture does not run into the path your finger has created, it means the mixture is cooked just right and 'coats the back of a spoon'.

VARQ

Varq, or edible silver foil, is very delicate and should be handled carefully. It is sold in sheets with a paper backing. To decorate with *varq*, carefully turn it over foil side down onto the *mithai* while it is still slightly warm. Press gently and peel away the paper layer, leaving the *varq* on the *mithai*.

Assorted Mithai

Burfi, Peda
&
Khoya Mithai

COCONUT BURFI

INGREDIENTS

2 cups grated fresh
coconut

1 cup (250 grams)
sugar

½ cup (100 ml)
fresh cream

A pinch of green
cardamom powder

2 tablespoons powdered
sugar

½ tablespoon ghee

This is my daughters'
favourite *burfi*. Add a
little cocoa and they
are in seventh heaven!

METHOD

Heat a non-stick pan on medium heat. Add the coconut,
sugar, cream and cardamom powder and cook, stirring
continuously, for fifteen minutes or till the mixture turns
a golden brown.

Remove from the heat and add the powdered sugar and mix.

Grease a *thali* with the ghee and pour in the coconut mixture
and spread evenly.

Cool and cut into diamonds or squares and serve.

Store in an airtight container in the refrigerator for up to
a week.

■ Makes 640 grams

Note

Fresh coconut has a short shelf life, so consume the *burfi*
as soon as possible.

BANANA HALWA BURFI

INGREDIENTS

1 cup chopped ripe bananas (Nendra Bale/Nendrapazham)

1 cup (180 grams) grated *khoya/mawa*

½ cup (125 grams) sugar

Ghee for greasing

½ cup coarsely ground cashew nuts

¼ cup (50 ml) milk

Ripe bananas cooked with *khoya* and served *burfi*-style. Down south, especially in Kerala and Karnataka, they make this sweet using the special Nendra Bale or Kerala bananas, which have a flavour unmatched by any other.

METHOD

Grease a six-by-eight-inch straight-sided shallow tray with a little ghee.

Place a non-stick pan on medium heat. Add the bananas and grated *khoya*; cook, stirring at regular intervals to prevent the mixture from scorching.

Cook till the ghee begins to ooze from the mixture. Add the sugar and cashew nut powder, and mix. Continue to cook, stirring continuously, till the mixture turns a rich brown. Add the milk and cook till it starts leaving the sides of the pan.

Pour the mixture into the greased tray, level the surface and set aside to cool. Cut into desired shapes and serve.

■ Makes 250 grams

BESAN BURFI

METHOD

Heat the ghee in a non-stick *kadai*; add the gram flour and sauté on low heat, stirring continuously, for ten to fifteen minutes, or till it starts changing colour and is fragrant.

Add the cardamom powder and pistachio and almond slivers, and mix. Remove from the heat and set aside to cool.

Add the powdered sugar and mix well.

Grease a six-by-eight-inch aluminium straight-sided shallow tray with the ghee. Pour the gram flour mixture into the tray and spread it evenly with a greased spatula.

Cool and cut into squares or diamonds and serve.

Store the *burfi* in an airtight container.

■ Makes 300 grams

INGREDIENTS

2 cups (200 grams) gram flour

½ teaspoon green cardamom powder

10-12 pistachios, cut into thin slivers

10-12 almonds, cut into thin slivers

1 cup (125 grams) powdered sugar

1 cup (200 ml) melted pure ghee + for greasing

You can whip up this rich dried fruit and besan *burfi* flavoured with cardamom in no time at all.

GAJAR HALWA BURFI

METHOD

Grease a six-by-eight-inch aluminium tray.

Heat the ghee in a non-stick pan. Add the carrots and sauté till the moisture is absorbed.

Add the sugar and mix. Cook, stirring frequently, till the carrots are soft and the moisture is absorbed.

Add the cardamom powder, condensed milk and *khoya*, and mix. Cook till the *khoya* melts and the mixture thickens. Add the raisins and mix.

Pour the mixture into the greased tray and spread evenly. Sprinkle the almonds and pistachios, and set aside to cool. Alternatively, place in a refrigerator to set.

Cut into squares or diamonds and serve.

■ Makes 600 grams

INGREDIENTS

5 large carrots, thickly grated

4 tablespoons ghee, at room temperature + for greasing

1 cup (250 grams) sugar

1 teaspoon green cardamom powder

½ tin (200 grams) condensed milk

1 cup (180 grams) *khoya/mawa*, grated

18-20 raisins

10-12 almonds, blanched, peeled and slivered

10-12 pistachios, blanched, peeled and slivered

The famous and favourite *gajar halwa* turned into a *burfi*... easy to cook, easy to eat and easy to store! But I must say it tastes best when eaten fresh.

KAJU-KESAR BURFI

INGREDIENTS

4 cups (500 grams)
cashew nut powder

A few saffron threads

2 cups (500 grams)
sugar

1 tablespoon milk

1 tablespoon liquid
glucose

¼ teaspoon liquid
yellow food colour

¼ teaspoon liquid
orange food colour

1 teaspoon ghee, for
greasing

2-3 sheets of edible
silver foil (see note on
page 7)

This burfi made
with cashew nuts
and flavoured with
saffron is ideal for
festive occasions! I like
presenting it as a gift,
especially at Diwali.

METHOD

Cook two cups of water with the sugar in a deep non-stick pan, stirring till the sugar dissolves. Add the milk and collect the scum, which rises to the surface with a ladle, and discard. Cook till the syrup attains multi-string or hard-ball consistency (see note on page 7).

Take the pan off the heat, add the cashew nut powder and mix well. Add the liquid glucose and mix well.

Add the saffron and the food colours, and continue to mix till the mixture is smooth and pliable.

Transfer the mixture onto a flat surface and spread to cool a bit. Knead with the heel of your hands.

Grease a table top with ghee and roll out the mixture to about half a centimetre thickness, taking care that the same thickness is maintained throughout.

Rub the surface with butter paper. Decorate with silver foil, cut into diamonds and serve.

■ Makes 950 grams

CHOCOLATE BURFI

METHOD

Cook the *khoya* and sugar together in a large non-stick *kadai* on low heat, stirring continuously till the sugar dissolves and the *khoya* starts to melt.

Add the liquid glucose and continue to cook for about twenty minutes, stirring continuously, till the mixture thickens and begins to leave the sides of the *kadai*. Add the cardamom powder and mix well.

Divide the mixture into two parts. Add two teaspoons of cocoa powder to one part and mix well.

Transfer the cocoa mixture onto a greased six-by-eight-inch aluminium tray and spread it evenly. Leave to cool to room temperature and set.

Spread the remaining *khoya* mixture on top of the chocolate layer and spread it evenly. Set aside to cool. Cut into twenty squares or diamonds and serve with the chocolate layer on top.

■ Makes 20 pieces/400 grams

INGREDIENTS

2 teaspoons
cocoa powder

2 cups + 1 tablespoon
(375 grams) *khoya/
mawa*

½ cup (125 grams)
sugar

1 teaspoon liquid
glucose

A pinch of green
cardamom powder

Try this *burfi* once,
and you will keep
coming back for more.

SEV BURFI

INGREDIENTS

250 grams unsalted *sev*

2¾ cups (500 grams) *khoya/mawa*

1 cup (250 grams) sugar

2 teaspoons milk

A few drops of yellow food colour

1 cup (200 ml) milk

3-4 drops of rose essence

10-12 pistachios, chopped

10-12 almonds, chopped

10-12 cashew nuts, chopped

A Sindhi favourite, *Singhar ji Mithai* as it is traditionally known, is popular with just about everyone else as well.

METHOD

Cook the sugar with one and a half cups of water in a non-stick pan, stirring till the sugar melts. Add the milk, collect the scum, which rises to the surface with a ladle, and discard. Add the food colour and mix. Lower the heat and add the *sev*. Mix gently so that the *sev* does not get mashed.

Add the *khoya* and mix. Add the milk and cook till the mixture thickens. Add the rose essence and mix. Add half the pistachios, almonds and cashew nuts, and mix gently.

Grease a six-by-eight-inch aluminium tray and pour the mixture into it. Level the surface and sprinkle the remaining pistachios, almonds and cashew nuts.

Set aside to cool. When completely cold, cut into squares and serve.

■ Makes 750 grams

MAWA BURFI

INGREDIENTS

2 cups + 1 tablespoon (375 grams) *khoya/ mawa*

½ cup (125 grams) sugar

1 teaspoon liquid glucose

A pinch of green cardamom powder

Looking for the perfect festive delicacy? This is the answer. Simple, easy to make and so delicious, it disappears in the blink of an eye!

METHOD

Cook the *khoya* and sugar together in a large thick-bottomed non-stick *kadai* on low heat, stirring continuously, till the sugar dissolves and the *khoya* starts to melt.

Add the liquid glucose and continue to cook, stirring continuously, for twenty minutes, or till the mixture thickens and begins to leave the sides of the *kadai*. Add the cardamom powder and mix well.

Transfer the mixture to a greased six-by-eight-inch aluminium tray and spread evenly. Set aside to cool to room temperature and set. Cut into twenty squares or diamonds and serve.

- 20 *mawa burfi*/400 grams

TIL BURFI

INGREDIENTS

1 cup (160 grams) sesame seeds

3 tablespoons pure ghee, at room temperature

1½ cups (270 grams) *khoya/mawa*, grated

½ cup (125 grams) sugar

5-6 almonds, chopped

5-6 pistachios, chopped

A delightful combination of crisp sesame seeds, crunchy nuts and soft *khoya* – can you get more festive than that!

METHOD

Heat a non-stick pan; add the sesame seeds and dry-roast till light pink. Set aside to cool. Grease an eight-by-six-inch tray. Heat the ghee in a non-stick *kadai*. Add the *khoya* and sauté on low heat till light pink and fragrant.

Add the roasted sesame seeds and sugar, and continue to sauté for three to four minutes or till the sugar dissolves completely. Add the chopped nuts and mix well.

Transfer to the greased *thali*, level the surface and set aside to cool. Cut into desired shapes and serve. Store in an airtight container when completely cooled.

- Makes 400 grams

KESAR BURFI

Cook the *khoya* and sugar together in a large non-stick *kadai* on low heat, stirring continuously till the sugar dissolves and the *khoya* starts to melt.

Add the liquid glucose and continue to cook, stirring continuously. Add the yellow and orange colours, and mix well. Cook for twenty minutes, or till the mixture thickens and begins to leave the sides of the *kadai*.

Sprinkle cardamom powder and saffron, and mix well.

Transfer the mixture onto a greased six-by-eight-inch aluminium tray and spread it evenly. Leave to cool to room temperature and set.

Cut into twenty squares or diamonds, decorate with silver foil, and serve.

- Makes 20 pieces/440 grams

A few saffron threads

2 cups + 1 tablespoon (375 grams) *khoya/ mawa*

½ cup (125 grams) sugar

1 teaspoon liquid glucose

¼ teaspoon liquid yellow food colour

⅛ teaspoon liquid orange food colour

A pinch of green cardamom powder

Edible sliver foil, as required (see note on page 7)

Try this classic *khoya mithai* with the richness of saffron – yellow-orange diamonds decorated with silver foil makes these a feast for the eye.

MALAI PEDA

INGREDIENTS

1 litre whole milk

A few saffron threads

4 teaspoons milk

½ cup (125 grams) sugar

2 pinches of citric acid

1 teaspoon cornflour

¼ teaspoon green cardamom powder

4-5 almonds, chopped

7-8 pistachios, chopped

This has to be everyone's favourite *peda* and ideal for that quick sweet fix!

METHOD

Bring the milk to a boil in a deep non-stick pan. Cook, stirring continuously, for about twenty minutes, till it reduces to half its original volume.

Soak the saffron in two teaspoons of warm milk and add to the boiling milk.

Add the sugar and continue to cook for four to five minutes.

Mix the citric acid in one tablespoon of water and add gradually to the boiling milk. Cook till the milk curdles slightly.

Mix the cornflour with the remaining two teaspoons of milk and add to the pan. Cook, stirring continuously, for about forty-five minutes till the mixture thickens and resembles *khoya*.

Add the cardamom powder and mix well.

Remove from heat and set aside to cool. Divide into sixteen equal portions and shape into round balls. Decorate with almonds and pistachios, and serve.

■ Makes 16 *peda*

CHOCOLATE PEDA

INGREDIENTS

2 tablespoons cocoa powder

2 cups + 1 tablespoon (375 grams) *khoya/ mawa*

½ cup (125 grams) sugar

⅛ teaspoon liquid chocolate food colour

10–12 almonds, slivered

Chocolate insinuates itself into every confection, including *peda*. No one can eat just one!

METHOD

Cook the *khoya* with sugar in a non-stick pan, stirring continuously, for about twenty minutes, or till the mixture begins to leave the sides of the pan.

Remove the pan from the heat, add the cocoa powder and chocolate colour, and mix well. Set aside to cool.

Divide the mixture into sixteen equal portions and shape them into *peda*.

Decorate with almond slivers and set aside for one whole day to set before serving.

■ Makes 16 *peda*/400 grams

KESARI PEDA

METHOD

Cook the *khoya* and sugar together in a large non-stick *kadai* on low heat, stirring continuously, till the sugar dissolves and the *khoya* starts to melt.

Add the liquid glucose and continue to cook, stirring continuously. Add the yellow and orange colour, and mix well. Cook for twenty minutes or till the mixture thickens and begins to leave the sides of the *kadai*.

Sprinkle the cardamom powder and saffron, and mix well.

Let the mixture cool sufficiently so that you can handle it. Divide into sixteen equal portions and shape each one into a *peda*. Place a pistachio slice on each *peda* and press lightly.

■ Makes 16 *peda*/400 grams

INGREDIENTS

A few saffron threads

2 cups + 1 tablespoon (375 grams) *khoya/ mawa*

½ cup (125 grams) sugar

1 teaspoon liquid glucose

¼ teaspoon liquid yellow food colour

⅛ teaspoon liquid orange food colour

A pinch of green cardamom powder

A few pistachios, sliced

Saffron-flavoured *peda* bejewelled with pistachios — a visual and gastronomical delight!

MATHURA KA PEDA

METHOD

Sauté the *khoya* in a non-stick pan on medium heat, stirring continuously, for eight to ten minutes. Take the pan off the heat and set aside to cool.

Cook the sugar with one-fourth cup water in another non-stick pan on medium heat, stirring till the sugar dissolves. Add the milk and collect the scum, which rises to the surface with a ladle, and discard.

Cook till the syrup attains a one-string consistency (see note on page 7). Add the liquid glucose and stir well. Take the pan off the heat.

Add the *khoya* mixture to the sugar syrup and mix well. Transfer the mixture to a bowl.

Divide the mixture into twelve equal portions and shape into round balls. Press the balls lightly.

Spread the caster sugar in a plate and roll the *peda* lightly in it. Arrange on a serving dish and serve.

■ Makes 12 *peda*

INGREDIENTS

2 cups (360 grams) *khoya/mawa*

¼ cup (60 grams) sugar

1 teaspoon milk

¼ teaspoon liquid glucose

¼ cup (35 grams) caster sugar

Originating in the holy city of Mathura, these *peda* are divine in more ways than one!

GULAB JAMUN

INGREDIENTS

¾ cup (125 grams) *hariyali khoya/mawa* (see note on page 6)

½ cup (60 grams) cottage cheese (*malai paneer*)

3½ tablespoons refined flour

3½ tablespoons cornflour

1½ cups (375 grams) sugar

1 teaspoon milk

¼ teaspoon green cardamom powder

Ghee for deep-frying

This is one of those recipes for an all-time favourite that you can master in minutes. Just follow the steps exactly and you will be rewarded with soft, luscious *jamun* floating in a pool of liquid gold.

METHOD

Grate the *khoya* and cottage cheese separately and mix together in a bowl.

Add the refined flour and cornflour, and knead well till smooth. Divide into twenty-five equal portions.

Place each portion of the *khoya*-cottage cheese mixture in your palm, press and roll into a smooth ball. Ensure there are no cracks on the surface.

To make the syrup, cook the sugar with one and one-fourth cups of water, stirring till the sugar dissolves. Add the milk and collect the scum, which rises to the surface with a ladle, and discard. Add the cardamom powder and simmer till the syrup turns a light golden. Keep the syrup warm.

Heat sufficient ghee in a non-stick *kadai* on medium heat. Gently slide in half the *khoya* balls. Lift the *kadai* off the heat and place on a heatproof board on the worktop; rotate the *kadai* gently till the balls float to the top.

Place the *kadai* back on the heat and continue to fry on medium heat, stirring gently, till the balls turn golden brown.

Remove the *jamun* with a slotted spoon and soak in the syrup for at least fifteen minutes before serving.

Serve warm or cold.

■ Makes 25 *gulab jamun*

MAWA-ANJEER BURFI

METHOD

Cook the *khoya* and sugar together in a large non-stick *kadai* on low heat, stirring continuously, till the sugar dissolves completely, and the *khoya* starts to melt.

Add the liquid glucose and continue to cook, stirring continuously, for thirteen minutes, or till the mixture thickens and begins to leave the sides of the *kadai*. Add the almonds, cashew nuts and dried figs, and mix well.

Transfer the mixture to a greased six-by-eight-inch aluminium tray and spread it evenly. Leave to cool to room temperature. Cut into squares and serve.

- Makes 420 grams

INGREDIENTS

2 cups + 1 tablespoon
(375 grams) *khoya/
mawa*

7-8 dried figs, chopped

½ cup (125 grams)
sugar

1 teaspoon liquid
glucose

5-6 almonds, chopped

5-6 cashew nuts,
chopped

Crunchy, chewy and
velvety - a trio of
sensations in one bite!

STUFFED GULAB JAMUN

METHOD

Grate the *khoya* and cottage cheese separately and mix.

Reserve two tablespoons of the *khoya* mixture. Add the refined flour and cornflour to the remaining mixture and knead well till smooth. Divide into twenty-five equal portions.

Add the crushed pistachios and cardamom powder to the reserved *khoya-paneer* mixture and mix well. Divide into twenty-five equal portions and roll into balls.

Take each portion of the *khoya-paneer* mixture in your palm, make a hollow in the centre and place the *khoya*-pistachio mixture in it. Bring the edges together to seal the filling, press and roll into a smooth ball. Ensure no cracks form.

Boil together the sugar and one and one-fourth cups of water, stirring till the sugar dissolves. Add the milk, collect the scum, which rises to the surface with a ladle, and discard. Simmer till the syrup turns a light golden. Keep the syrup warm.

Heat sufficient ghee in a *kadai* on medium heat. Gently slide in half the *khoya* balls. Lift the *kadai* off the heat and rotate it gently till the balls float to the top.

Place the *kadai* back on the heat and continue to fry on medium heat, stirring gently, till the *jamun* turn golden brown in colour.

Drain and place them in the syrup. Let them soak for at least fifteen minutes before serving.

Serve warm or cold.

■ Makes 25 *jamun*/750 grams

INGREDIENTS

¾ cup (125 grams) *hariyali khoya/mawa* (see note on page 6)

½ cup (60 grams) cottage cheese (*malai paneer*)

3½ tablespoons (25 grams) refined flour

3½ tablespoons (20 grams) cornflour

5-6 pistachios, crushed

¼ teaspoon green cardamom powder

Syrup

1½ cups (375 grams) sugar

1 teaspoon milk

Ghee for deep-frying

All the sumptuousness of a *gulab jamun* and more – a rich *khoya* and pistachio filling which takes it to a whole new level of gustatory pleasure.

MAWA MODAK

INGREDIENTS

2 cups + 1 tablespoon (375 grams) *khoya/mawa*

½ cup (125 grams) sugar

1 teaspoon liquid glucose

A pinch of green cardamom powder

Mawa lovingly shaped into Lord Ganesha's favourite *modak* – sweet devotion!

METHOD

Cook the *khoya* and sugar together in a large non-stick *kadai* on low heat, stirring continuously, till the sugar dissolves completely and the *khoya* starts to melt.

Add the liquid glucose and continue to cook, stirring continuously, for twenty minutes, or till the mixture thickens and begins to leave the sides of the *kadai*.

Add the cardamom powder and mix well. Remove from the heat and set aside to cool to room temperature.

Divide the mixture into sixteen equal portions and shape into modak. Alternatively, shape the mixture in a *modak* mould and serve.

■ Makes 16 *modak*/400 grams

KALA JAMUN

Grate the *khoya* and cottage cheese separately and mix.

Add the refined flour and cornflour, and knead well till smooth. Divide into twenty-five equal portions. Take each portion in your palm, press and roll into a smooth ball. Ensure there are no cracks on the surface.

To make the syrup, bring the sugar and one and one-fourth cups of water to a boil, stirring till the sugar dissolves. Add the milk. Collect the scum, which rises to the surface with a ladle, and discard. Add the cardamom powder and simmer till the syrup turns a light golden. Keep the syrup warm.

Heat sufficient ghee in a non-stick *kadai* on medium heat. Gently slide in half the *khoya* balls. Lift the *kadai* off the heat and place on the worktop; rotate it gently till the balls float to the surface.

Place the *kadai* back on the heat and continue to fry on medium heat, stirring gently, till they turn dark brown in colour.

Drain and dip them in the syrup. Let them soak for at least fifteen minutes before serving. Decorate with silver foil. Serve warm or cold.

- Makes 25 *kala jamun*/ 1.25 kg

Black is beautiful as you will see when you fry regular *gulab jamun* till they turn a fierce black, but lose none of their sumptuous charm!

¾ cup (125 grams) *hariyali khoya/mawa* (see note on page 6)

½ cup (60 grams) cottage cheese (*malai paneer*)

3½ tablespoons refined flour

3½ tablespoons cornflour

1½ cups (375 grams) sugar

1 tablespoon milk

¼ teaspoon green cardamom powder

Ghee for deep-frying

Edible silver foil, as required (see note on page 7)

Assorted Mithai

Laddoo, Katli
&
Rolls

RAGHAVDAS LAADOO

INGREDIENTS

½ cup grated fresh coconut

1½ cups (300 grams) fine semolina

⅜ cup (75 ml) pure ghee

1½ cups (375 grams) sugar

1 tablespoon milk

½ teaspoon green cardamom powder

2-3 tablespoons raisins

During the festival of Ganesh Chaturthi, these *laddoo* are offered as *naivedyam* to the Lord. Quick and simple to prepare they can be stored easily, if only they didn't vanish ever so fast!

METHOD

Roast the coconut in a non-stick *kadai* on medium heat for six minutes or till reddish brown. Transfer to a bowl and set aside.

Add the ghee to the same *kadai*. Add the semolina and sauté, stirring continuously, for fifteen minutes or till light brown. Take the *kadai* off the heat, add the coconut and stir well.

Add the cardamom powder and stir well. Add the raisins, reserving a few for decoration, and stir.

In another non-stick pan, cook the sugar with three-fourth cup of water, stirring till the sugar dissolves. Add the milk, collect the scum, which rises to the surface with a ladle, and discard. Cook to make a syrup of one-string consistency (see note on page 7).

Add the semolina mixture and mix well. Cover and set aside for fifteen minutes till the mixture cools a little.

Grease your palms with a little ghee and shape into twenty-five *laddoo*. Decorate each *laddoo* with a raisin.

When completely cooled store in an airtight container.

- Makes 25 *laddoo*/700 grams

Note

These *laddoo* contain fresh coconut and should be consumed as soon as possible.

CHURMA LADDOO

INGREDIENTS

2 cups coarse wholewheat flour

4 tablespoons ghee + for deep-frying

¾ cup grated jaggery

¼ cup (30 grams) powdered sugar

1 teaspoon green cardamom powder

1 teaspoon nutmeg powder

Poppy seeds, as required

Alas, you cannot eat more than one or two of these *laddoo* so rich and full of flavour, as they are loaded with ghee!

METHOD

Place the flour in a bowl; add two tablespoons of hot ghee and gently rub it in with your fingertips. Add sufficient warm water and knead into a stiff dough. Divide the dough into four equal portions and shape into small *muthia* (oval-shaped croquettes).

Heat sufficient ghee in a non-stick *kadai* and deep-fry the *muthia* till golden brown. Drain on absorbent paper, break into smaller pieces and set aside to cool.

When completely cool, grind the *muthia* to a powder. Pass the powder through a sieve. Grind the residue remaining in the sieve to a fine powder and add to the sifted powder.

Heat two tablespoons of ghee in another non-stick pan. Add the jaggery and cook, stirring, till it melts. Remove from the heat and add the sifted *muthia* flour and mix well. Add the powdered sugar and mix. Add the cardamom powder and nutmeg powder, and mix well.

Divide the mixture into sixteen equal portions and shape each portion into a *laddoo*. Roll the *laddoo* in the poppy seeds. Cool and store in an airtight container.

■ Makes 16 *laddoo*/480 grams

KURMURA LADDOO

METHOD

Heat a non-stick pan; add the ghee and jaggery, and cook till the syrup attains a soft-ball consistency (see note on page 7).

Add the puffed rice and mix.

Divide into equal portions and shape into *laddoo*.

- Makes 125 grams

INGREDIENTS

2 cups coarse

2 cups puffed rice

½ cup (100 grams) jaggery, grated

1 tablespoon ghee

Punjabis look forward every year to *Lohri* which celebrates the end of winter with bonfires, folk songs and *kurmura laddoo!*

KAJU, KHOYA AUR BESAN KE LADDOO

METHOD

Melt the ghee in a non-stick *kadai* and add the gram flour. Cook on low heat, stirring, for about fifteen to twenty minutes till the gram flour is light brown and fragrant. Add the cardamom powder, stir and take the pan off the heat. Let the mixture cool for a while.

Add half a cup of powdered sugar and mix well with your hands. Cool again and divide into twelve equal portions. Shape each portion into a *laddoo*.

Sauté the *khoya* in another non-stick *kadai* for four to five minutes. Add the remaining powdered sugar and cashew nut powder. Divide into twelve equal portions.

Take each portion of the *khoya* mixture and spread it thickly on your palm. Place a gram flour *laddoo* in the centre, gather the edges of the *khoya* together and roll, making sure that the gram flour *laddoo* is completely covered with the *khoya* mixture.

Set aside to cool completely and store in an airtight container.

INGREDIENTS

½ cup (125 grams) cashew nuts, coarsely powdered

2 cups (360 grams) *khoya/mawa*

½ cup (50 grams) gram flour

¼ cup (55 grams) ghee

½ teaspoon green cardamom powder

1 cup (125 grams) powdered sugar

I am usually at my creative best when I am cooking for my family and close friends. This particular *laddoo* became such a hot favourite with them, that I felt I must share the recipe with you.

MOTICHOOR LADDOO

½ cup + 2 tablespoons (60 grams) gram flour

A few saffron threads (optional)

¾ cup (185 grams) sugar

2 teaspoons milk

Oil for deep-frying

5-6 pistachios, slivered

This confection of a multitude of tiny golden gram flour pearls fused into a syrupy ball, is a North Indian contribution to the Indian *mithai* platter.

Mix together the gram flour and half a cup plus one tablespoon of water in a large bowl. Whisk well to make a smooth batter of pouring consistency.

Pass the mixture through a strainer into another bowl. Add the saffron, mix well and set aside.

Cook the sugar with half a cup of water in a deep non-stick pan, stirring till the sugar dissolves. Add the milk, and when the scum rises to the surface, collect it in a ladle and discard. Cook the syrup till it attains a one-string consistency (see note on page 7).

Heat sufficient oil in a non-stick *kadai* on medium heat. Dip a perforated spoon, with small holes, into the batter; shake off the excess batter and tap the spoon on the rim of the *kadai* so that small *boondi* fall into the hot oil. Quickly gather these *boondi* with another perforated spoon and put them into the sugar syrup. Continue the process with the rest of the batter.

Leave the *boondi* to soak in the sugar syrup for an hour, till soft.

Squeeze out the excess sugar syrup and shape them into sixteen lemon-sized *laddoo*.

Serve the *laddoo* garnished with pistachio slivers.

■ Makes 16 *laddoo*/400 grams

CHOCO-COCONUT LADDOO

Place two cups of desiccated coconut in a bowl. Add the almonds, walnuts and pistachios, and mix. Set aside.

Melt the chocolate in a microwave-safe bowl in a microwave oven on **HIGH** (100%) for one minute.

Remove from the microwave oven and whisk till smooth. Add to the desiccated coconut mixture.

Add the condensed milk and mix well. Shape into small balls. Roll the balls in the remaining desiccated coconut and arrange on a plate.

Store the *laddoo* in an airtight container in the refrigerator.

- Makes 550 grams

1 cup grated chocolate

2½ cups desiccated coconut

½ cup almonds, chopped

¼ cup walnuts, crushed

¼ cup pistachios, coarsely ground

3 tablespoons sweetened condensed milk

Press a button, wait a minute, swirl and roll, and voilà you have a batch of sweet temptations on a platter.

TILACHE LADDOO

INGREDIENTS

¾ cup (120 grams) white sesame seeds

½ cup grated dried coconut

¼ cup (35 grams) roasted Bengal gram

¼ cup (30 grams) peanuts, roasted and coarsely ground

A pinch of green cardamom powder

½ cup (125 grams) jaggery (*chikki gur*), grated

1 tablespoon ghee

'Til-gul ghya, gode gode bola' – an exhortation to sweeten one's mouth and one's speech, with these sesame and jaggery *laddoo* at Makar Sankranti, the harvest festival in Maharashtra.

METHOD

Dry-roast the sesame seeds in a non-stick pan on low heat till light brown. Remove from the pan and set aside in a bowl.

Dry-roast the dried coconut in the same pan on low heat till light brown. Add to the sesame seeds in the bowl and mix. Add the roasted Bengal gram and roasted peanuts, and mix. Add the cardamom powder and mix. Keep the mixture warm.

Heat the ghee in a non-stick pan. Add the jaggery and cook till it attains a soft-ball consistency (see note on page 7).

Add the sesame seed mixture and mix well. Divide the mixture into thirty equal portions and roll them into round *laddoo* while the mixture is till hot.

Cool completely and store in an airtight container.

- Makes 30 *laddoo*/450 grams

Note

Laddoo should be rolled when the mixture is still hot, as the mixture starts solidifying as it cools. *Tilache laddoo* should be crisp and firm and one can store them in an airtight container for fifteen days or longer.

BADAM KATLI

INGREDIENTS

250 grams almonds

¾ cup (190 grams) sugar

1 tablespoon milk

1¼ teaspoons liquid glucose

1-2 sheets edible silver foil (see note on page 7)

My father's eyes would light up at the sight of these pale diamonds swathed in silver.

METHOD

Blanch the almonds in two cups of boiling water for five minutes. Drain and peel. Spread the almonds on an absorbent kitchen towel to dry.

Dry-roast the almonds in a non-stick frying pan or *tawa* for about seven minutes, or till fragrant and light brown. Cool and grind to a fine powder. You should have 190 grams of ground almonds.

Cook the sugar with three-fourth cup water in another non-stick pan, stirring continuously till the sugar dissolves. Add the milk. Collect the scum, which rises to the surface with a ladle, and discard. Continue to cook till the syrup reaches multi-thread or hard-ball consistency (see note on page 7). Take the pan off the heat.

Add the ground almonds and liquid glucose, and mix well till the mixture is smooth and pliable. Transfer the mixture onto a flat surface and spread out till cool enough to knead the mixture with your hands.

Grease a work surface with the ghee and roll out the mixture into a one-fourth-inch thick uniform square or rectangle. Rub the surface with butter paper to make it smooth so the silver foil will stick to it. Decorate with the silver foil, cut into diamonds and serve.

- Makes 375 grams

METHOD

Cook the sugar with one and one third cups of water in a deep non-stick pan, stirring till the sugar dissolves.

Add the milk, and when the scum rises to the top collect it with a ladle, and discard. Continue cooking over medium heat for twelve minutes, or till it attains a multi-string consistency (see note on page 7).

Stir in the liquid glucose and ghee.

Remove the pan from the heat and add the pistachio powder, stirring vigorously. Knead lightly to make a soft dough.

Grease a ten-by-eight-inch aluminium tray and spread the dough in it. Smooth the surface with a sheet of butter paper.

Gently spread the silver foil over the top and cut into twenty diamonds. Store in an airtight container when cool.

- Makes 20 *pista katli*/960 grams

INGREDIENTS

$4\frac{1}{6}$ cups (approx. 500 grams) pistachio powder

$1\frac{1}{3}$ cups (335 grams) sugar

1 tablespoon milk

2 tablespoons liquid glucose

$1\frac{1}{2}$ tablespoons ghee

Edible sliver foil, as required (see note on page 7)

Pistachios provide a richer more intense flavour than the traditional cashew nut to this popular *mithai*.

KAJU-PISTA-BADAM-KESAR BURFI

METHOD

Soak the saffron in one tablespoon of warm water and set aside.

Heat a non-stick pan. Add the *khoya*, sugar and glucose, and cook for fifteen minutes, or till the *khoya* leaves the sides of the pan.

Remove from the heat and divide into four portions.

Add the cashew nuts to one portion, almonds to the second portion, pistachios to the third portion and saffron to the fourth. Mix each portion well.

Grease a two-inch deep, six-inch square aluminium tray with a little ghee. Divide each portion of *burfi* again into four portions and shape each one into a cylinder.

Starting from left to right first, lay a cylinder each of cashew nut, almond, pistachio and saffron *burfi*. Starting from left to right again, place a cylinder each of saffron, pistachio, almond and cashew nut *burfi* over the first layer. Place another layer in the first order. Repeat with a layer of the *burfi* in the order of the second layer.

Gently tap the tray on the tabletop and leave to set. Cut into squares and serve.

■ Makes 440 grams

INGREDIENTS

10 cashew nuts, coarsely ground

10 pistachios, coarsely ground

10 almonds, coarsely ground

A few saffron threads

2 cups +1 tablespoon (375 grams) *khoya/ mawa*

½ cup (125 grams) sugar

1 teaspoon liquid glucose

Ghee, for greasing

Too much of a good thing can be delicious, you will discover when you bite into this saffron-flavoured *mithai* laden with dried fruit.

PISTA ROLL

INGREDIENTS

1½ cups (185 grams) pistachios

⅔ cup (85 grams) sugar

1 tablespoon liquid glucose

1 tablespoons ghee

Edible silver foil, as required (see note on page 7)

Sink your teeth into these pastel green nutty confections for that perfect sweet bite.

METHOD

Blanch, drain and peel the pistachios. Roast them in the oven and then powder coarsely.

Cook the sugar with two and a half cups of water in a deep non-stick pan over medium heat till the syrup reaches 118°C/244°F, or till it attains a multi-string consistency (see note on page 7).

Stir in the liquid glucose and ghee.

Remove the pan from the heat and add the pistachio powder, stirring continuously. Knead lightly to make a soft dough.

Divide the mixture into two equal portions and roll them out as thinly as possible. Roll each one up into a long cylinder and cut into one-inch pieces.

Decorate with silver foil and arrange the rolls on a platter. Place in a refrigerator to set for an hour before serving.

- Makes 350 grams

KAJU-PISTA ROLL

Blanch the pistachios in two cups of hot water for five minutes. Drain, peel and grind coarsely.

Cook the *khoya* in a non-stick pan, stirring continuously, for about ten minutes. Set aside to cool. Add the cashew nut powder and sugar, and knead to a smooth mixture.

Divide the mixture into two equal parts. To one part add the coarsely powdered pistachios and cardamom powder.

Take half the plain cashew nut mixture and roll it into a four-by-five-inch rectangle.

Take half a portion of the pistachio mixture and roll it into a five-inch long cylinder. Place it at one end of the cashew nut rectangle and roll up the cashew nut sheet enclosing the pistachio roll.

Use the remaining cashew nut and pistachio mixtures to make a similar roll. Gently press silver foil on the rolls. Cut into two-inch pieces and serve.

■ Makes 600 grams

2 cups (250 grams) cashew nut powder

1 cup (125 grams) pistachios

$1^2/_5$ cup (250 grams) *khoya/mawa*

1⅓ cups (165 grams) powdered sugar

¼ teaspoon green cardamom powder

2 sheets edible silver foil (see note on page 7)

Mithai on a roll – or two rolls - one delicious roll inside the other. As someone said, 'nothing succeeds like excess'!

Assorted Mithai

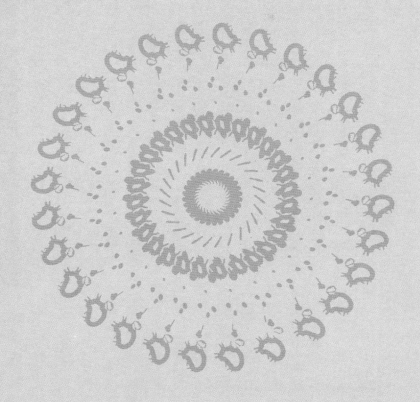

Chhena & Paneer
Mithai

CHUM CHUM

Boil the milk on high heat. Set aside to cool slightly (77°C/170°F).

Mix the vinegar in one and three-fourth cups of water and add to the hot milk. Stir lightly till the milk curdles. Add three to four cups of cold water and a few ice cubes and stir.

Strain the *chhena* through a piece of muslin and squeeze to remove all the water. You should have 250 grams of *chhena*. Transfer the *chhena* onto a worktop. Mix together half a teaspoon of refined flour and the cornflour, and add to the *chhena*. Knead with the heel of your hands to a smooth mixture.

Divide the mixture into twenty-five equal portions and roll into oblong smooth rolls, taking care that there are no cracks. Make a small dent on one side and set aside. Mix the remaining flour with half a cup of water and set aside.

To make the syrup, cook the sugar with five cups of water, stirring continuously till the sugar dissolves. Add the milk and let the syrup come to a boil. Collect the scum, which rises to the surface with a ladle and discard. Continue to cook the syrup for a few minutes longer. Strain the syrup into a bowl.

Pour one cup of the syrup into a deep, wide non-stick pan and add four to five cups of water. When the syrup comes to a boil, add the *chhena* rolls and half the flour-water mixture. The syrup will start frothing. Let the rolls cook in the syrup. Do not stir, but gently agitate the syrup so that the balls do not stick to the bottom of the pan.

Slowly drizzle half a cup of water along the sides of the pan every five minutes to prevent the syrup from thickening and forming strings. Continue cooking for fifteen minutes, or till the rolls spring back to their original shape.

Drain the rolls and soak in the reserved syrup. Chill for at least two hours so that the syrup is absorbed by the *chhena* rolls. For the topping, cook the *khoya* with the rose water, saffron, sugar syrup and yellow colour till the mixture thickens to the consistency of jam.

Take the *chhena* balls out of the syrup, spread a little of the *khoya* mixture into the hollows and serve.

■ Makes 25 *chum chum*

Chhena

10 cups (2 litres) cow's milk

8 teaspoons (40 ml) white vinegar

1 tablespoon refined flour

½ teaspoon cornflour

Syrup

4⁴/₅ cup (1.2 kg) sugar

2 tablespoons milk

Topping

2 tablespoons (40 grams) *khoya/mawa*

1 teaspoon rose water

3-4 saffron threads

1 tablespoon sugar syrup

A small pinch or a few drops of edible yellow colour

The Bengalis do it best – use *chhena* to fashion a variety of spongy delights that squirt sweetness with every bite. Add creamy *khoya*, and one can look forward to double the delight.

55

ROSOGULLA

INGREDIENTS

Chhena

10 cups (2 litres)
cow's milk

8 teaspoons (40 ml)
white vinegar

1 tablespoon refined
flour

½ teaspoon cornflour

Syrup

4⁴/₅ cups (1.2 kg) sugar

2 tablespoons milk

Both Bengal and Orissa
lay claim to creating this
masterpiece. With this
never-fail recipe you too
can create a work of art
– or many works of art,
based on this pristine,
succulent sphere.

METHOD

For the *chhena*, bring the milk to a boil over high heat. Set aside to cool slightly to 77°C/170°F. Mix the vinegar in one and three-fourth cups of water and add to the hot milk. Stir lightly till the milk curdles. Add three to four cups of water and a few ice cubes and stir.

Strain the *chhena* through a piece of muslin and squeeze to remove all the water. You should have 250 grams of *chhena*.Transfer the *chhena* onto a worktop. Mix together half teaspoon of refined flour and the cornflour, and add to the *chhena*. Knead, pressing with the heel of your hand, till the mixture is smooth. Divide into twenty-five portions of ten grams each and roll into balls taking care that there are no cracks. Mix the remaining refined flour with half a cup of water and set aside.

To make the syrup, cook the sugar with five cups of water, stirring continuously till all the sugar dissolves. Add the milk and let the syrup come to a boil. Collect the scum, which rises to the surface with a ladle, and discard. Continue to cook the syrup for a few minutes longer. Strain the syrup into a bowl.

Take one cup of the syrup, reserving the rest, in a deep, wide non-stick pan and add four to five cups of water. When the syrup begins to boil add the *chhena* balls. Add half the flour mixture. The syrup will froth. Cook, gently agitating the syrup so that the balls do not stick to the bottom of the pan.

Slowly drizzle half a cup of water along the sides of the pan every five minutes so that the syrup does not thicken. Continue cooking for fifteen minutes or till the *chhena* patties spring back when pressed. This is a sign that they are cooked.

Remove the balls with a slotted spoon and place in the reserved syrup. Chill for at least two hours so the *rosogulla* absorb the syrup. Serve.

- Makes 25 *rosogulla*/ 1.25 kg

Note

For mini *rosogulla*, shape the *chhena* mixture into smaller balls.

CHHENA MURKI

METHOD

For the syrup, cook the sugar with one cup of water, stirring continuously, till the sugar dissolves. Add the milk. Collect the scum, which rises to the surface with a ladle, and discard. Cook the syrup till it attains a one-string consistency (see note on page 7).

Add the cottage cheese and cook till the syrup coats the cubes well.

Remove from heat, add the screw pine essence and mix well. Keep swirling the pan till the cubes are thickly coated with the syrup and separated from each other.

Arrange in a serving plate and sprinkle liberally with icing sugar.

- Makes 300 grams

INGREDIENTS

250 grams cottage cheese, cut into ½-inch cubes

1 cup (250 grams) sugar

1 tablespoon milk

2-3 drops screw pine essence

Icing sugar, for dusting

A Bengali creation – paneer cubes with a thick sugary crust – sweet perfection!

SANDESH

INGREDIENTS

8 cups (1.6 litres) milk

¼ cup lemon juice

½ cup (65 grams) caster sugar

A pinch of green cardamom powder

12 pistachios, blanched and finely chopped

Bengalis love their mishti and melt-in-the mouth 'shondesh' has pride of place in their pantheon of sweet delights.

METHOD

Bring the milk to a boil in a deep, thick-bottomed non-stick pan. Add the lemon juice and stir till the milk curdles. Strain and immediately refresh the *chhena* in chilled water.

Put the *chhena* in a piece of muslin and squeeze till all the water is drained out.

Knead the *chhena* well with the heel of your hand. Add the caster sugar and cardamom powder, and knead again.

Cook in a non-stick pan on medium heat for eight minutes. Remove from heat and divide into twelve equal portions. Roll each portion into a ball and make a dent on the top.

When cooled, place a pistachio in the dent and serve.

- Makes 12 *sandesh*/350 grams

KHEER KADAM

METHOD

Squeeze the mini *rosogulla* to remove excess sugar syrup.

Grate two cups of *khoya* finely. Add the powdered sugar and knead into a smooth dough.

Place a non-stick frying pan on high heat; add the *khoya*-sugar mixture and sauté for four to five minutes. Transfer to a bowl and set aside to cool. When cool, add the rose essence and knead well.

Divide the *khoya* mixture into sixteen equal portions and shape into balls. Make small hollows in the centre with your thumb. Thin the edges and place a mini *rosogulla* in each hollow. Cover the *rosogulla* completely with the *khoya* so that no part of it is left exposed. Roll once again into balls.

Grind the remaining *khoya* to a powder. Roll the balls in the powdered *khoya*. Store in a refrigerator and serve chilled.

■ Makes 16 *kheer kadam*/400 grams

INGREDIENTS

16 mini *rosogulla* (page 56)

2 cups + 3 tablespoons (420 grams) *khoya/ mawa*

4 tablespoons powdered sugar

½ teaspoon rose essence

As exotic and as indulgent as it can get - one sweet enclosing another!

RAJ BHOG

INGREDIENTS

Chhena

10 cups (2 litres)
cow's milk

8 teaspoons (40 ml)
white vinegar

1 tablespoon
refined flour

½ teaspoon cornflour

Filling

¼ cup (45 grams)
khoya/mawa

1 tablespoon pistachios

⅛ teaspoon green
cardamom powder

A few saffron threads

¼ teaspoon rose water

Syrup

4⁴/₅ cup (1.2 kg) sugar

2 tablespoons milk

A few saffron threads

A few drops of
yellow food colour

Glistening gold orbs
in a silvery sweet sea
– royally delicious!

METHOD

Bring the milk to a boil over high heat. Set aside to cool slightly to 77°C/170°F.

Mix the vinegar in one and three-fourth cups of water and add to the hot milk. Stir lightly till the milk curdles. Add three to four cups of water and a few ice cubes and stir.

Strain the *chhena* through a piece of muslin and squeeze to remove all the water. You should have 250 grams of *chhena*.

Transfer the *chhena* onto a worktop. Mix together half a teaspoon of refined flour and the cornflour, and add to the *chhena*. Knead, pressing with the heel of your hand, till the mixture is smooth.

Divide into twenty-five equal portions and roll into balls.

For the filling, grind together the *khoya*, pistachios, cardamom powder, saffron and rose water coarsely. Divide into twenty-five equal portions and roll into small balls.

Stuff each *chhena* ball with a portion of the filling and roll again into a ball taking care that no cracks form.

Mix the remaining refined flour with half a cup of water and set aside.

To make the syrup, cook the sugar with five cups of water, stirring continuously till the sugar dissolves. Add the milk and let the syrup come to a boil. Collect the scum, which rises to the surface with a ladle, and discard. Continue to cook the syrup for a few minutes longer. Strain the syrup into a bowl.

Pour one cup of the syrup, reserving the rest, into a deep and wide non-stick pan and add four to five cups of water.

When the syrup begins to boil add the *raj bhog*. Add half the flour-water mixture - the syrup will start frothing. Cook the *raj bhog*, gently agitating the syrup so that the balls do not stick to the bottom of the pan.

Slowly drizzle half a cup of water along the sides of the pan every five minutes so that the syrup does not thicken. Continue cooking for fifteen minutes or till the *raj bhog* spring back when pressed. This is a sign that they are cooked.

Add the saffron and yellow colour to the reserved syrup.

Remove the *raj bhog* from the cooking syrup with a slotted spoon and place in the saffron-flavoured syrup. Chill for at least two hours till the *raj bhog* absorb the syrup. Serve.

- Makes 25 *raj bhog*/ 1 kg

MALAI SANDWICH

Chhena

2 litres (10 cups)
cow's milk

8 teaspoons (40 ml)
white vinegar

1 tablespoon refined
flour

½ teaspoon cornflour

Syrup

4⁴⁄₅ cups (1.2 kg)
sugar

2 tablespoons milk

Filling

2 tablespoons (30
grams) *khoya/mawa*

1 teaspoon rose water

3-4 saffron threads

1 tablespoon sugar
syrup

A small pinch or a few
drops of yellow food
colour

*The sheer delight of
feasting on one of these
syrupy morsels makes all
the time and effort spent
worth it!*

Bring the milk to a boil on high heat. Set aside to cool slightly to about 77°C/170°F.

Mix the vinegar in one and three-fourth cups of water and add to the hot milk. Stir lightly till the milk curdles. Add three to four cups of water and a few ice cubes and stir. Strain the *chhena* through a piece of muslin and squeeze to remove the excess whey. You should have 250 grams of *chhena*.

Transfer the *chhena* onto a worktop. Mix together half a teaspoon of refined flour and the cornflour, and add to the *chhena*.

Knead, pressing with the heel of your hand, till the mixture is absolutely smooth. Divide into twelve equal portions and shape into squares, taking care that there are no cracks.

Mix the remaining refined flour with half a cup of water and set aside. To make the syrup, cook the sugar with five cups of water, stirring continuously till the sugar dissolves.

Add the milk and bring the syrup to a boil. Collect the scum, which rises to the surface with a ladle, and discard. Continue to cook the syrup for a few minutes longer. Strain the syrup into a bowl. Pour one cup of strained syrup, reserving the rest, into a deep, wide non-stick pan; add four to five cups of water and bring to a boil.

Add the *chhena* squares and half the flour mixture. The syrup will start frothing. Let the *chhena* squares cook. Do not stir but just agitate the syrup gently so that the squares do not stick to the bottom of the pan.

Slowly drizzle half a cup of water along the sides of the pan every five minutes so that the syrup does not thicken. Continue cooking for fifteen minutes longer, or till the *chhena* squares spring back when pressed. This is a sign that they are cooked.

Remove the *chhena* squares with a slotted spoon and place in the reserved syrup to soak. Place in a refrigerator to chill for at least two hours, or till the *chhena* squares absorb the syrup.

In a separate non-stick pan, cook the *khoya*, rose water, saffron, sugar syrup and yellow colour together till the mixture attains the consistency of jam. Divide the mixture into twelve equal portions.

Remove the *malai* squares from the syrup, slit each in half horizontally. Spread the *khoya* mixture on one half, place the other half over it and serve.

■ Makes 750 grams

KESARI INDRAYANI

METHOD

Bring the milk to a boil in a non-stick pan; lower the heat and simmer till the milk reduces to half its original volume. Add the cream, sugar and saffron, and cook till the sugar dissolves.

Squeeze the *rosogulla* to remove excess syrup and place them in a bowl. Pour the milk-cream mixture over and set aside to cool. When completely cold, place in a refrigerator to chill.

To serve, place a few chilled *rosogulla* in each bowl. Sprinkle the pomegranate kernels, grated *khoya*, pistachios and almonds on top and serve at once.

■ Makes 1.25 kg

This one's a favourite on our restaurant menu… tiny *rosogulla* soaked in rich and creamy saffron-flavoured milk…a magical treat, both for the eyes and the taste buds!

INGREDIENTS

A few saffron threads

20-25 mini *rosogulla* (page 56)

7½ cups (1½ litres) full cream milk

1 cup (200 ml) fresh cream

¾ cup (185 grams) sugar

½ cup fresh pomegranate kernels

½ cup (90 grams) *khoya/ mawa*, grated

8-10 pistachios, blanched, peeled and sliced

½ cup almonds, blanched and peeled

RASMALAI

INGREDIENTS

Chhena

10 cups (2 litres)
cow's milk

8 teaspoons (40 ml)
white vinegar

1 tablespoon refined
flour

½ teaspoon cornflour

Syrup

4⅘ cups (1.2 kg) sugar

2 tablespoons milk

Rabdi

10 cups (2 litres) milk

6 tablespoons
(90 grams) sugar

A few saffron threads

The word 'lip-smacking'
could have been
invented to describe *ras
malai*. And now with
the recipe at hand, you
can be smacking your
lips whenever the fancy
takes you!

METHOD

For the *chhena*, bring the milk to a boil over high heat. Set aside to cool slightly to 77°C/170°F.

Mix the vinegar in one and three-fourth cups of water and add to the hot milk. Stir lightly till the milk curdles. Add three to four cups of water and a few ice cubes and stir.

Strain the *chhena* through a piece of muslin and squeeze to remove all the water. You should have 250 grams of *chhena*.

Transfer the *chhena* onto a worktop. Mix together half teaspoon of refined flour and the cornflour, and add to the *chhena*. Knead, pressing with the heel of your hand, till the mixture is smooth.

Divide into twenty-five portions and roll into balls and then press lightly to make patties, taking care that there are no cracks.

Mix the remaining refined flour with half a cup of water and set aside.

To make the syrup, cook the sugar with five cups of water, stirring continuously till all the sugar dissolves. Add the milk and let the syrup come to a boil. Collect the scum, which rises to the surface, with a ladle and discard. Continue to cook the syrup for a few minutes longer. Strain the syrup into a bowl.

Take one cup of the syrup, reserving the rest, in a deep, wide non-stick pan and add four to five cups of water. When the syrup begins to boil add the *chhena* patties. Add half the flour-water mixture. The syrup will froth. Cook, gently agitating the syrup so that the balls do not stick to the bottom of the pan.

Slowly drizzle half a cup of water along the sides of the pan every five minutes so that the syrup does not thicken. Continue cooking for fifteen minutes or till the *chhena* patties spring back when pressed. This is a sign that they are cooked.

Remove from the syrup with a slotted spoon and place in the reserved syrup.

To make the *rabdi*, bring the milk to a boil in a deep, thick-bottomed non-stick pan on high heat Lower heat to medium and cook, stirring, till it reduces to three-fourth its original volume. Scrape off the cream that will collect on the sides of the pan and drop it back into the milk.

Add the sugar and saffron, and cook for five minutes longer. Transfer to a deep bowl.

Remove each *chhena* patty from the syrup, gently press to remove excess syrup and dip into the *rabdi*.

Chill for at least two hours so that the *chhena* patties absorb the *rabdi*. Serve.

- Makes 25 *rasmalai*/ 1.75 kg

Assorted Mithai

Sugar-Free Mithai

MAWA GUJIYA

INGREDIENTS

Pastry

1 cup (120 grams)
refined flour

3 tablespoons ghee

Oil for deep-frying

Filling

⅔ cup (120 grams)
khoya/mawa,
crumbled

½ cup (80 grams)
chopped dried figs

½ cup (75 grams)
chopped seedless
dates

10 cashew nuts,
chopped

10 almonds, chopped

10 walnuts, chopped

Why wait for Holi
to turn out these
gujiya packed with
the natural goodness
of dried fruit with no
added sugar?

METHOD

For the pastry, sift the flour into a bowl and rub in the ghee with your fingertips till the mixture resembles breadcrumbs. Add one-fourth cup and one tablespoon of cold water and knead into a stiff dough. Cover with a piece of damp muslin and set aside for fifteen minutes.

For the filling, heat a non-stick pan; add the *khoya* and sauté for three minutes or till the fat separates. Set aside to cool.

Add the figs, dates, cashew nuts, almonds and walnuts, and mix well. Divide into twelve equal portions.

Divide the dough into twelve equal portions and shape into balls. Roll out each ball into a *puri*. Place one portion of the stuffing on one half of the *puri*, lightly moisten the edges, fold the other half over the stuffing and press the edges to seal. Pinch the edges to make a design.

Heat sufficient oil in a non-stick *kadai*; gently slide in a few *gujiya* at a time, and deep-fry for five to six minutes or till golden brown.

Drain on absorbent paper and store in an airtight container when completely cold.

- Makes 12 *mawa gujiya*/720 grams

KHAJUR AUR AKHROT KA ROLL

INGREDIENTS

100 grams dates

50 grams walnuts

25 grams almonds

25 grams pistachios

25 grams figs

1 tablespoon ghee

1 tablespoon
(10 grams) edible
gum resin (gond)

1 sheet aluminium foil

2 tablespoons poppy
seeds

Who needs sugar when
you have real sweetness
in the mélange of dried
fruit packed into these
flavoursome rolls.

METHOD

Dry-roast the walnuts, almonds and pistachios. Coarsely chop the dates, walnuts, almonds, pistachios and figs.

Heat the ghee in a non-stick pan and add the gum resin. Shallow-fry the resin till the grains are swollen. Drain and crush or chop finely.

Heat the ghee remaining in the pan, add the chopped nuts and gum, and sauté till fragrant. Set aside to cool.

Knead the mixture into a dough, and spread it on a piece of aluminium foil. Tightly roll up the date mixture with the help of the foil and place in a refrigerator for about an hour.

Remove the foil and cut the nut roll into one-inch pieces. Roll in poppy seeds and serve.

- Makes 175 grams

KHAJURACHI WADI

METHOD

Coarsely grind the dates in a processor and transfer to a bowl. Coarsely grind the cashew nuts, almonds and pistachios.

Heat one tablespoon ghee in a non-stick pan, add the gum resin and shallow-fry till golden brown. Drain and set aside.

Add the remaining ghee to the same pan and sauté the cashew nuts, almonds, pistachios and poppy seeds. Add the dates and sauté till heated through.

Transfer to a plate and set aside to cool slightly.

Add the cardamom powder and nutmeg powder. Crush the gum resin and add. Mix well and knead into a dough.

Divide the mixture into two to three equal portions and shape into rolls. Wrap in aluminium foil and refrigerate for four to five hours.

Just before serving, unwrap the rolls and cut them into half-inch thick slices.

■ Makes 650 grams

INGREDIENTS

500 grams dates, seeded and chopped

¼ cup cashew nuts

¼ cup almonds

¼ cup pistachios

5 tablespoons ghee

2 tablespoons edible gum resin (gond), crushed

1 tablespoon poppy seeds, roasted

1 teaspoon green cardamom powder

½ teaspoon nutmeg powder

Aluminium foil, as required

The natural sugars in the dates suffuse these *mithai* with their sweetness.

STEAMED SANDESH

INGREDIENTS

8 cups (1.6 litres) milk

$\frac{1}{6}$ cup sugar
  substitute (sucralose)

$\frac{1}{4}$ cup lemon juice

A pinch of green
  cardamom powder

A generous pinch
  of saffron

1 tablespoon warm milk

12 pistachios, for
  decoration

It's a fresh, fun and a
deliciously different
version of the iconic
Bengali sweet. And
best of all - without the
calories of added sugar!

METHOD

Heat the milk in a deep non-stick pan. Bring to a boil, add the lemon juice and stir till the milk curdles. Strain and immediately refresh in chilled water.

Place the *chhena* in a piece of muslin and squeeze till all the water is drained out. Mix the saffron in one tablespoon of warm milk.

Knead the *chhena* well with your palms. Add the sugar substitute, cardamom powder and saffron-flavoured milk and knead again. Steam the mixture in a steamer for ten minutes.

When the mixture cools slightly, divide into twelve equal portions and shape each into an oval shape. When cooled decorate with pistachios and serve.

- Makes 12 *sandesh*/300 grams

BESAN KE LADDOO

INGREDIENTS

2 cups (200 grams)
coarse gram flour

6-8 cashew nuts

6-8 almonds

$\frac{1}{2}$ cup (115 grams) ghee

$\frac{1}{2}$ teaspoon green
cardamom powder

$\frac{1}{3}$ cup sugar substitute
(sucralose)

My father used to make
the most amazing *besan*
ke *laddoo*. He would
have been proud of this
version made with a sugar
substitute – perfect for
those for whom sugar is
the enemy.

METHOD

Coarsely grind together the cashew nuts and almonds, and set aside. Melt the ghee in a non-stick *kadai*. Add the gram flour and sauté on low heat till the gram flour is light brown and fragrant. This normally takes around fifteen to twenty minutes.

Add the cashew nuts, almonds and cardamom powder, stir to mix and take the *kadai* off the heat. Set aside to cool. Add the sugar substitute and mix well with your hands. Shape into walnut-sized balls and store in an airtight container when completely cooled.

- Makes 280 grams

Chef's Tip: Before serving besan ke *laddoo* that have been stored for a few days in the refrigerator, warm them for fifteen to twenty seconds in a microwave oven. They will not only become soft, but appear to be freshly made.

KESAR-PISTA PHIRNI

Bring the milk to a boil in a deep non-stick pan. Lower the heat and simmer, stirring continuously, till it reduces by half.

Add the rice flour, mixed with a little water, and stir well to prevent lumps from forming. Bring the mixture to a boil.

When it starts to thicken, lower the heat and simmer for a couple of minutes, stirring continuously. Add the cardamom powder and saffron, and mix well.

When the mixture attains a thick custard-like consistency, remove from heat and stir in the sugar substitute.

Pour the mixture into four individual earthenware bowls while still warm. Sprinkle sliced pistachios and refrigerate for at least two hours.

Serve chilled.

- Makes 600 grams

Chef's Tip: Sweet dishes with empty calories are a definite no-no for the calorie conscious. Therefore we have suggested the use of a sugar substitute. However, please check with your doctor before using it.

This legacy of Mughal cuisine has me enthralled. I find this sugar-free version of the silky smooth dessert particularly irresistible as it leaves me with no feelings of guilt!

A few saffron threads

10-12 pistachios, blanched, peeled and sliced

5 cups (1 litre) skimmed milk

3 tablespoons coarse rice flour

¾ teaspoon green cardamom powder

3 tablespoons sugar substitute (sucralose)

KESARI SHRIKHAND

INGREDIENTS

A generous pinch of saffron

1 kg yogurt

⅓ cup sugar substitute (sucralose)

2 tablespoons warm milk

A small pinch of nutmeg powder

¼ teaspoon green cardamom powder

5-6 almonds, blanched, peeled and sliced

8-10 pistachios, blanched, peeled and sliced

A dollop of this creamy, velvety dessert described as 'ambrosia of the gods', will definitely transport you to a celestial plane.

METHOD

Tie the yogurt in a piece of muslin and hang it overnight over a bowl, in a refrigerator, to drain.

Transfer the drained yogurt into a bowl. Add the sugar substitute and mix well.

Soak the saffron in warm milk, cool and add to the yogurt mixture. Mix well.

Add the nutmeg powder and cardamom powder; mix well and chill in the refrigerator.

Serve chilled, decorated with the almonds and pistachios.

■ Makes 500 grams

MANGO BURFI

METHOD

Cook the mango pulp in a non-stick pan on medium heat, stirring continuously, for ten minutes, or till it reduces to half its original quantity.

Boil the milk in a deep thick-bottomed non-stick pan, stirring continuously, for eight minutes, or till it thickens slightly.

Add the alum and the mango pulp, and stir continuously till the milk becomes grainy.

Cook for twenty minutes, or till most of the moisture evaporates and a solid mass remains.

Add the sugar substitute and mix well.

Grease a six-by-eight-inch aluminum tray with ghee. Pour the mango mixture into the tray and level the surface. Sprinkle the sliced almonds on top. Leave to set for an hour in a cool, dry place.

Cut into squares or diamonds, and serve.

■ Makes 625 grams

INGREDIENTS

1 cup mango pulp

10 cups (2 litres) buffalo milk

¼ teaspoon alum (*phitkari*), crushed

4 teaspoons sugar substitute (sucralose)

½ tablespoon pure ghee

20 almonds, thinly sliced

Got milk? And mangoes? Make *burfi*! Stir up a batch and indulge your passion for the king of fruit in its *mithai* avatar without the guilt of added sugar.

Assorted Mithai

Mithai Platter

LAVANG LATIKA

INGREDIENTS

Pastry

1 cup refined flour

3 tablespoons ghee +
for deep-frying

12 cloves

Filling

3 tablespoons
khoya/mawa

2 tablespoons assorted
nuts (cashew nuts
and almonds)

1 tablespoon
powdered sugar

¼ teaspoon green
cardamom powder

A few saffron threads

Syrup

1 cup (250 grams) sugar

2 teaspoons milk

One of Bengal's most
popular sweets…crisp
pastry packages stuffed
with *khoya* and nuts,
fastened with a clove
and soaked in a warm
sugar syrup, is proof
enough that the best,
and sweetest, things
come in small packages!

METHOD

For the pastry, place the flour in a bowl and rub in the ghee
with your fingertips. Add sufficient water and knead into a
stiff dough. Cover with a damp cloth and rest the dough for
a while.

For the syrup, cook the sugar with half a cup of water in a
non-stick pan, stirring continuously till the sugar dissolves.
Add the milk; collect the scum, which rises to the surface
with a ladle, and discard. Cook the syrup till it attains a
one-string consistency (see note on page 7). Remove from
heat and keep warm.

For the filling, mix together the *khoya*, nuts, powdered
sugar, cardamom powder and saffron. Divide the mixture
into twelve equal portions.

Divide the dough into twelve equal portions. Roll out each
portion into a five-inch round *puri*.

Place one portion of the filling in the centre of the *puri*, fold
in the sides to overlap each other and seal the ends with a
little water. Secure with a clove.

Heat sufficient ghee in a non-stick *kadai* and deep-fry the
lavang latika till golden brown. Drain on absorbent paper.

Soak the *lavang latika* in the warm sugar syrup for three to
four minutes.

Drain and serve warm..

- Makes 400 grams

DHODA

INGREDIENTS

10 cups (2 litres) milk

⅛ teaspoon alum (*phitkari*)

³⁄₅ cup (150 grams) sugar

2 tablespoons liquid glucose

2 tablespoons ghee

¼ cup assorted nuts (cashew nuts, almonds, pistachios), chopped

One of Punjab's traditional *mithai*, *dhoda's* richness is symbolic of the verdant land of milk and honey.

METHOD

Bring the milk to a boil in a large non-stick *kadai* on high heat. Add the alum and sugar, and continue to cook, stirring continuously, for about one and a half hours, or till the milk becomes grainy and begins to thicken.

Add the glucose and stir well. Add the ghee and cook for a few minutes longer, stirring continuously, till the mixture begins to leave the sides of the *kadai*.

Sprinkle four tablespoons of water and stir. Cook, stirring continuously, till the mixture turns brown.

Transfer onto a ten-by-eight-inch greased tray and tap the tray on the tabletop to spread it evenly. Sprinkle the nuts and leave to set for four to five hours before cutting into squares.

- Makes 750 grams

ANGOORI PETHA

METHOD

Cut the ash gourd into wedges, peel and remove the seeds. Prick the wedges all over with a needle. Mix the lime powder in three litres of water and soak the ash gourd wedges in it for two to three hours.

Remove and wash the wedges thoroughly under running water at least three to four times. Cut the wedges into half-inch cubes.Alternatively, cut the wedges into small cylinders with a cylinder-shaped cutter.

Mix together four cups of sugar and four and a half cups of water in a deep non-stick pan and bring to a boil. Add four tablespoons of milk. When the scum rises to the top, collect it with a ladle, and discard.

Add one cup of water and bring the mixture to a boil again. Add the ash gourd and cook on low heat for forty to forty-five minutes, or till completely cooked and translucent.

Meanwhile, dissolve the remaining sugar in one and a half cups of water and bring it to a boil. Add the remaining milk. When the scum rises to the top, collect it with a ladle, and discard. Continue cooking to make a syrup of one-string consistency (see note on page 7).

Strain the syrup into a clean bowl; add the rose essence and mix. Add the cooked ash gourd and leave to soak overnight in the syrup and serve.

■ *Makes 600 grams*

Note

You can add saffron to the syrup to make *kesari angoori petha*.

INGREDIENTS

1.5 kg ash gourd

$5/6$ cup (180 grams) slate lime powder (*chuna*)

6 cups (1.5 kg) sugar

5 tablespoons milk

A few drops of rose essence

No, there are no grapes in this sweet. It is just a variation of Agra's most famous *mithai*.

MILK POWDER GULAB JAMUN

INGREDIENTS

4 cups (560 grams) milk powder

1 cup (120 grams) refined flour

A pinch of soda bicarbonate

2 teaspoons oil + for deep-frying

Yogurt, as required

Syrup

4 cups (1 kg) sugar

1 teaspoon green cardamom powder

METHOD

Cook the sugar with four cups of water in a non-stick pan till the sugar dissolves. Add the cardamom powder and mix. Keep the syrup warm.

Mix together the milk powder, refined flour and soda bicarbonate. Add two teaspoons of oil and enough yogurt, and knead lightly into a soft dough. Do not over-knead the dough. Divide the dough into sixteen marble-sized balls.

Heat sufficient oil in a non-stick *kadai* and deep-fry the balls over medium heat, stirring occasionally, till golden brown.

Drain on absorbent paper. Add the *gulab jamun* to the warm syrup and leave to soak for about fifteen minutes to half an hour before serving.

- Makes 16 *gulab jamun*/ 800 grams

This is one of those short cuts for an instant dessert that one relishes for its speed and simplicity.

CHANDRAKALA

INGREDIENTS

Pastry

1 cup (120 grams) refined flour

A pinch of salt

1½ tablespoons ghee + for deep-frying

Filling

¾ cup (135 grams) grated *khoya/mawa*

½ cup (65 grams) caster sugar

METHOD

For the pastry, sift together the flour and salt into a bowl. Rub in one and a half teaspoons of ghee and knead into a firm dough using water as required. Cover with a damp cloth and set aside.

For the filling, cook the *khoya* in a non-stick pan on low heat, stirring continuously, for three to four minutes.

Add the caster sugar, almonds, cashew nuts and cardamom powder, and remove from heat. Set aside to cool.

For the syrup, cook the sugar with one and one-fourth cups of water in a non-stick pan, stirring till the sugar dissolves.

Add the milk and collect the scum, which rises to the surface with a ladle, and discard. Cook till the syrup attains a one-thread consistency (see note on page 7). Add the saffron and stir. Keep the syrup hot.

Divide the dough into twenty equal portions. Roll out each portion into a three-inch *puri*. Take two *puri* at a time. Place one tablespoon of *khoya* filling in the centre of one *puri*, moisten the edge and cover with the other *puri*. Pinch or twist the edges in a pattern to seal firmly.

Heat sufficient ghee in a non-stick *kadai* and deep-fry the *chandrakala*, on medium heat, till golden brown. Drain and soak immediately in the hot syrup.

When the *chandrakala* are coated on all sides with the sugar syrup, gently remove and serve.

■ Makes 20 *chandrakala*/600 grams

Note

Chandrakala are made in half-moon shapes in South India.

6 almonds, coarsely powdered

6 cashew nuts, coarsely powdered

½ teaspoon green cardamom powder

Syrup

1¼ cups (310 grams) sugar

1 tablespoon milk

A few saffron threads

Who can blame you for throwing caution to the wind this Holi when presented with these irresistible calorie-laden treats?

CHOCOLATE-WALNUT FUDGE

INGREDIENTS

100 grams dark
chocolate, grated

½ cup walnuts,
finely chopped

4 tablespoons
unsalted butter

1 tin (400 grams)
sweetened condensed milk

1 cup (180 grams)
khoya/mawa, grated

½ teaspoon vanilla essence

METHOD

Grease a seven-inch square aluminium tray.

Heat a non-stick pan; add the butter and allow it to melt.
Add the chocolate and stir till it melts. Stir in the condensed
milk and cook for five to six minutes.

Add the walnuts to the pan and mix. Add the grated *khoya*,
and vanilla essence, and mix well.

Transfer the mixture onto the greased tray and spread evenly
with a greased spatula.

Cool in the refrigerator before cutting into pieces. Serve
chilled.

■ Makes 750 grams

Fudge is giving
burfi some serious
competition, especially
in the hill-stations,
where culinary vestiges
of the Raj still remain.

BALUSHAHI

METHOD

Sift together the flour and soda bicarbonate into a large bowl. Rub four tablespoons of ghee into the flour mixture with your fingertips till it resembles breadcrumbs.

Add the beaten yogurt and knead into a soft dough. Cover the dough with a damp cloth and allow it to rest for forty-five minutes.

Divide the dough into twelve equal portions and shape into smooth balls. Take care not to overwork the dough. Make a slight dent in the centre of the ball with your thumb. Keep the balls covered.

Heat sufficient ghee in a non-stick *kadai* on medium heat. Gently slide in the prepared dough balls, two to three at a time, and deep-fry on low heat. If necessary, place a non-stick *tawa* below the *kadai* so that the ghee does not get too hot.

Gradually the *balushahi* will start floating to the top. Turn gently and fry the other side till golden. The entire process may take around half an hour to forty-five minutes. Remove with a slotted spoon and drain on absorbent paper. Set aside to cool for forty-five minutes, or till they reach room temperature.

Cook the sugar with one cup of water in a deep non-stick pan on high heat, stirring occasionally, till the sugar dissolves. Add the milk to the cooking syrup. Collect the scum, which rises to the surface with a ladle, and discard. Continue to cook till the syrup attains a two-string consistency (see note on page 7).

Remove the syrup from heat and soak the cooled *balushahi* in it for two hours.

Gently remove the *balushahi* from the sugar syrup and place on a serving plate. Decorate with the pistachios. Set aside for two to three hours till the sugar syrup forms a thin white coating on the *balushahi*.

- Makes 12 *balushahi*

INGREDIENTS

1½ cups (180 grams) refined flour

¼ teaspoon soda bicarbonate

4 tablespoons pure ghee + for deep-frying

6 tablespoons yogurt, whisked till smooth

2 cups (500 grams) sugar

2 tablespoons milk

4–5 pistachios, finely chopped

I remember as a young boy I used to devour these delectable sweets, resembling glazed doughnuts, by the dozen!

GHEVAR

METHOD

Mix together the flour, cornflour and melted ghee in a bowl. Add one cup of water in a thin stream and whisk continuously so that all the ingredients blend well, and the ghee and water emulsify into a smooth mixture and do not separate.

Add two more cups of water in a thin stream and whisk continuously to ensure again that the ghee and water do not separate. The batter should be of coating consistency (see note on page 7). If necessary, add some more water to get the right consistency. Keep the batter in a cool place away from heat, but not in a refrigerator.

In a non-stick pan, cook the sugar with half a cup of water, stirring till the sugar dissolves. Add the milk. Collect the scum, which rises to the surface with a ladle, and discard. Cook till the syrup attains a one-string consistency (see note on page 7). Stir in the screw pine essence. Remove from heat and keep warm.

Pour sufficient ghee in a non-stick *kadai* and place a three-and-a half-inch round, 2-inch high mould in the centre, so that three-fourth of the height of the mould is immersed in the ghee. Heat the ghee on medium heat.

Pour three ladlefuls of the batter into a small bowl, add a pinch of soda bicarbonate and mix well. When the ghee is hot enough, pour one ladle of batter into the centre of the mould in a thin stream.

When the froth settles down, pour in another ladle of batter into the mould in a thin stream. When the froth settles down, make a hole in the centre of the *ghevar* with a thin wooden skewer or satay stick and pour another ladleful of batter into the hole.

Increase the heat and cook the *ghevar*, ladling the hot ghee over it two to three times. When the centre is firm and cooked, gently pull out the *ghevar* from the mould with a wooden skewer inserted in the centre. Hold it over the *kadai* till most of the ghee drains away. Immerse in the sugar syrup for twenty minutes. Drain and place on a platter. Decorate with the sliver foil and almonds. Cool and serve.

■ Makes 500 grams

INGREDIENTS

1¾ cup (210 grams) refined flour

1 tablespoon cornflour

¼ cup (45 grams) melted ghee, at room temperature

1 cup (250 grams) sugar

1 tablespoon milk

A few drops of screw pine essence

Soda bicarbonate, as required

Ghee for deep-frying

Edible silver foil, as required (see note on page 7)

8 almonds, slivered

This Rajasthani filigreed delicacy is usually prepared during Teej and Rakhi festivals. The elaborate processes in preparing it may seem daunting, but if you persevere you will be rewarded with a lacy creation that will fill your guests with awe.

BOMBAY HALWA

INGREDIENTS

¾ cup + 1 tablespoon
(200 grams) sugar

1 teaspoon lemon juice

3⅓ tablespoons
(50 grams) cornflour

6½ tablespoons (100
grams) ghee

A pinch or a few drops
of edible colour
(yellow, green or
orange)

1 teaspoon green
cardamom powder

½ cup cashew nuts

This firm chewy *halwa*
is also known as *Karachi
halwa* – creating some
confusion about its
origins. But, a *halwa* by
any other name will taste
as delicious!

METHOD

Boil the sugar with half a cup plus five teaspoons of water
and the lemon juice. Mix the cornflour with half a cup of
water till smooth.

Pour one tablespoon of ghee into a non-stick pan. Add the
cornflour mixture and cook on low heat, stirring continuously.
When the mixture begins to thicken, remove from heat and
add the sugar syrup, a little by little, till all the syrup is used
up. Keep stirring to prevent lumps from forming.

Place back on low heat and add the remaining ghee, a little
by little, stirring continuously, till all the ghee is used up.
Add the colour and cardamom powder, and cook for fifteen
to twenty minutes, or till the ghee separates.

Add the cashew nuts and mix well. Transfer onto a greased
six-by-eight-inch aluminium tray and spread evenly with a
greased spatula. Cut into squares or diamonds, and remove
when completely cooled.

- Makes 250 grams

GUAVA CHEESE

Cut the guavas into four equal pieces and remove the seeds. Put the seeds in a sieve and pressing with a flat spoon so that all the pulp surrounding the seeds is extracted. Transfer the pulp into a bowl.

Blend the guava pieces to a smooth pulp and add the pulp removed from the seeds. You should have 2 cups of guava purée.

Grease a six-by-eight-inch aluminium tray.

Transfer the guava purée to a non-stick pan and place on medium heat. Add the sugar and cook, stirring continuously, for twenty minutes or till the mixture thickens and begins to leave the sides of the pan. By this time, the mixture will become quite hard to stir.

Transfer the mixture onto the greased tray and spread evenly. Level the top with a greased spatula. When it cools a little cut into squares or diamonds.

Cool and store in an airtight container.

- Makes 250 grams

1 kilogram soft ripe guavas, peeled

1 cup (250 grams) sugar

A chewy fudge-like sweet, it is best made with fresh guavas. A popular Goan delicacy that can either be had for breakfast as a spread on hot toasts when not fully cooked, or cook it till it can be cut into squares and eat it as a dessert.

JALEBI

INGREDIENTS

1½ cups + 2 tablespoons (195 grams) refined flour

¼ teaspoon liquid yellow or orange food colour

2 cups (500 grams) sugar

1 tablespoon milk

½ teaspoon green cardamom powder

2 cups (425 grams) pure ghee

Jalebi and milk for breakfast in North India, or *jalebi* with *fafda, kadhi* and *papaya* chutney in Gujarat, or just *jalebi* – the anytime, anywhere snack - these crisp coils of sweetness provide one with instant gratification.

METHOD

Place the refined flour in a bowl, add one and a half cups of water and beat with your hands for half an hour to make a light smooth batter. Cover the bowl and keep in a warm place to ferment for twenty hours.

Beat the batter again with your hands for fifteen minutes. Add the food colour and two tablespoons of refined flour and beat again for ten minutes.

Cook the sugar with two cups of water in a deep non-stick pan on high heat, stirring continuously, till the sugar dissolves. Add the milk, collect the scum, which rises to the surface with a ladle, and discard.

Add the cardamom powder and cook, stirring, till the syrup attains a one-string consistency (see note on page 7). Let the syrup cool, but ensure that it remains lukewarm.

Heat the ghee in a non-stick frying pan on medium heat. Pour some of the batter into a squeeze bottle. Hold the bottle over the hot ghee and gently squeeze the batter into the ghee in spiral shapes. Start from the outside and work inwards for better results.

Cook, gently turning the *jalebi* over occasionally, for eight minutes on each side or till golden and crisp. Drain and soak in the sugar syrup for two to three minutes.

Drain and serve hot.

■ Makes 30 *jalebi*

Chef's Tip: Traditionally *jalebi* are fried in a special wide, shallow pan called a *jalebi tawi*. The batter is squeezed through a *jalebi* cloth, which is a piece of thick cloth with a three millimetre hole in the centre. *Jalebi*-making takes some practice and patience. To start with, try making individual *jalebi* and when you have perfected that, try making them together in a row. To make crisper *jalebi*, add a little rice flour to the refined flour.

GUR PARE

METHOD

Melt the jaggery in one-fourth cup of warm water and stir till completely dissolved. Strain to remove impurities.

Place the refined flour in a deep bowl; add the melted jaggery, fennel seeds and melted *vanaspati* and knead into a medium soft dough. Cover the dough with a damp cloth and let it rest for some time.

Sprinkle some refined flour on a flat surface and roll out the dough into a one-fourth-inch thick *chapati*. Cut into diamond-shaped pieces.

Heat sufficient oil in a non-stick *kadai*. Gently slide in the pieces, a few at a time, and deep-fry till golden brown.

Drain on absorbent paper. Serve hot, or store in an airtight container when completely cooled.

■ Makes 450 grams

INGREDIENTS

½ cup (100 grams) grated jaggery

1⅔ cups (200 grams) refined flour + for dusting

2 teaspoons fennel seeds, coarsely ground

¼ cup *vanaspati*, melted

Oil for deep-frying

Jaggery replaces sugar in these crisp sweet diamonds. They make a welcome contrast to a platter filled with rich, soft *mithai*.

GURPAPDI

INGREDIENTS

1¼ cups (250 grams) grated jaggery

2 cups (300 grams) wholewheat flour

1 cup ghee (225 grams) + 2 teaspoons for greasing

¼ teaspoon green cardamom powder

A generous pinch of nutmeg powder

Something special for Sankranti – a traditional, rustic *mithai* that celebrates the harvest.

METHOD

Heat one cup of ghee in a non-stick *kadai* and add the flour. Cook, stirring continuously, on medium heat for fifteen to twenty minutes, or till fragrant and brown.

Remove from the heat and add half the cardamom powder. Mix well. After five to six minutes add the jaggery and mix till well blended.

Grease a *thali* with two teaspoons of ghee. Transfer the mixture to the *thali* and spread evenly. Mix together the remaining cardamom powder and nutmeg powder, and sprinkle over the *gurpapdi*.

Leave to set at room temperature. Cut into squares or diamonds, and serve.

- Makes 320 grams

PARWAL KI MITHAI

INGREDIENTS

250 grams pointed gourd (*parwal*), peeled, slit and seeded

1 cup (180 grams) *khoya/mawa*

1¼ cups (310 grams) sugar

¼ teaspoon green cardamom powder

10 almonds, chopped

10 pistachios, chopped

METHOD

To make the filling, roast the *khoya* in a non-stick pan on medium heat till soft. Add one-fourth cup sugar and continue to cook.

Add the cardamom powder to the *khoya* mixture and mix. Take the pan off the heat; add the almonds and pistachios, and mix. Add the milk powder and mix well. Transfer the mixture onto a plate and leave to cool.

In a separate non-stick pan, bring the remaining sugar and one cup of water to a boil, stirring till the sugar dissolves. Add the milk, collect the scum, which rises to the surface with a ladle, and discard. Simmer for a few minutes longer to make a thin sugar syrup.

Heat plenty of water in a deep non-stick pan; add a pinch of soda bicarbonate and the *parwal* and boil for two to three minutes.

Drain and place the *parwal* in the sugar syrup. Cook for fifteen minutes, or till they soften. Drain and set aside to cool.

Stuff the the *parwal* with the *khoya* mixture. Sprinkle a few saffron threads over each *parwal* and decorate with silver foil.

Serve cold.

■ Makes 400 grams

2 tablespoons milk powder

2 teaspoons milk

A pinch of soda bicarbonate

A few saffron threads

Edible silver foil, to decorate (see note on page 7)

Who would believe that a humble gourd could be transformed into a treat for the taste buds? But steeped in a sugary bath and filled with a rich mixture of nuts and *khoya* it is pure pleasure on a plate.

UKDICHE MODAK

INGREDIENTS

1½ cups (225 grams)
Basmati rice flour

A pinch of salt

1 teaspoon oil +
for greasing

Stuffing

1½ cups grated
fresh coconut

1 cup (200 grams)
grated jaggery

1 tablespoon roasted
poppy seeds

A pinch of green
cardamom powder

A pinch of nutmeg
powder

Lord Ganesh loves
these little steamed
dumplings made of a
translucent rice flour
pastry stuffed with a
mixture of sweetened
coconut and jaggery.
And I do too!

METHOD

Heat one and one-fourth cups of water with salt and one
teaspoon oil in a deep non-stick pan.

Bring to a boil, reduce heat, and add the rice flour in a steady
flow, stirring continuously to prevent lumps from forming.
Cover the pan with a deep lid and pour some water into the
lid. Cook on low heat for three minutes.

Remove the lid, sprinkle some cold water on the rice flour
and cover again with the lid with water in it; cook for another
three minutes. Repeat this process twice more. Take the
pan off the heat and keep it covered for two minutes.

Transfer the mixture to a large plate (*parat*), grease the
palms of your hands with oil and knead the dough till
completely smooth and pliable. The dough should not stick
to your palms. Rest the dough covered with a damp cloth.

For the stuffing, combine the coconut and jaggery in a non-
stick pan and cook on medium heat for one or two minutes
till light golden brown. Make sure that you do not overcook
the mixture. Add the roasted poppy seeds, cardamom
powder and nutmeg powder, and mix well. Remove from
heat and set aside to cool. Divide the coconut mixture into
twelve equal portions.

Divide the dough into twelve equal portions and shape them
into balls. Grease the palms of your hands and spread each
ball to form a three-inch bowl. Press the edges of the bowls
to reduce the thickness.

Place a portion of the stuffing in the centre; pleat the edges
of the dough and gather them together to form a bundle.
Pinch to seal the edges at the top.

Heat sufficient water in a steamer. Place the *modak* on a
perforated plate in the steamer and steam for ten to twelve
minutes. Serve hot *modak* with pure ghee.

■ Makes 12 *modak*

KUNDA

INGREDIENTS

2 cups + 1 tablespoon (375 grams) *khoya/ mawa*

½ cup (125 grams) sugar

¼ cup yogurt, whisked

10–12 almonds, split

10–12 cashew nuts, split

I learned how to make this traditional sweet in Belgaum from a sweet maker. I was surprised to see how easy it is to make it and am happy to share the recipe with you.

METHOD

Cook the *khoya* and sugar together in a large non-stick *kadai* on low heat, stirring continuously, till the sugar dissolves completely, and the *khoya* starts to melt.

Add the yogurt and continue to cook for thirty minutes, stirring continuously, till the mixture thickens and begins to leave the sides of the *kadai*.

Add the almonds and cashew nuts, and mix well. Transfer the mixture to a greased six-by-eight-inch aluminium tray and spread it evenly.

Leave to cool to room temperature and serve.

- Makes 400 grams

KALAKAND

Boil the milk in a large non-stick *kadai* on high heat. Add the alum and sugar, and continue to cook, stirring continuously, for about one and a half hours, or till the milk becomes grainy and begins to thicken.

Add the ghee and glucose; mix well and continue to cook till the mixture begins to coat the back of the ladle.

Transfer the mixture into a greased ten-by-eight-inch aluminium tray, sprinkle the pistachios and set aside to cool and set.

Cut into squares and serve.

- Makes 600 grams

10 cups (2 litres) milk

⅛ teaspoon alum

³⁄₅ cup (150 grams) sugar

2 tablespoons ghee

2 tablespoons liquid glucose

20 pistachios, finely chopped

Who can resist rich milky granules compacted into squares of sweet satisfaction.

MALPUA

INGREDIENTS

1 litre + 3 teaspoons milk

1¼ cups (310 grams) sugar

6-8 saffron threads

¼ cup refined flour

1 tablespoon semolina

Pure ghee for shallow-frying

These sugar-soaked pancakes are most popular in Bihar, Bengal and Maharashtra. They are even eaten at breakfast to kickstart the day! Try them with *rabdi* for a truly decadent dessert!

METHOD

Bring one litre milk to a boil in a deep, thick-bottomed non-stick pan on high heat. Lower the heat to medium and simmer, stirring frequently, till the milk reduces to a consistency that coats the back of a spoon (see note on page 7). Set aside to cool.

Soak the saffron in one teaspoon of hot milk.

Reserve two tablespoons of sugar. Place the remaining sugar in another deep thick-bottomed non-stick pan; add half a cup of water and cook, stirring occasionally. Add two teaspoons of milk to the syrup. Collect the scum, which rises to the surface with a ladle, and discard. Cook till the sugar syrup reaches one-string consistency (see note on page 7).

Add the saffron-flavoured milk to the sugar syrup.

Add the refined flour, semolina and the reserved sugar to the cooled thickened milk. Mix well to make a batter of pouring consistency, adding a little milk if required. Set aside for three hours. Do not place the batter in the refrigerator.

Place a wide non-stick frying pan on high heat and pour in the ghee. Pour a ladleful of batter and spread lightly into a round pancake. Spoon the hot ghee over the pancake and cook for one minute; turn the pancake over. Cook, turning, till both sides are cooked and golden brown. Drain and immerse in the sugar syrup for at least fifteen minutes.

Remove and serve warm.

- Makes 600 grams

MILK CAKE

METHOD

Bring the milk to a boil in a large thick-bottomed non-stick *kadai* on high heat. Add the alum and sugar, and continue to cook, stirring continuously, for about one and a half hours, or till the milk becomes grainy and begins to thicken.

Add the ghee and liquid glucose; mix well and continue to cook till the mixture begins to leave the sides of the *kadai*.

Transfer the mixture to a seven-and-a-half-inch round and two-and-a-half-inch deep greased dish and cover it. Set aside for four to five hours. During this time it will continue to cook and the middle layer will become light brown.

Turn the milk cake out onto a serving dish, cut into squares and serve.

■ Makes 730 grams

INGREDIENTS

10 cups (2 litres) milk

⅛ teaspoon alum

³/₅ cup (150 grams) sugar

2 tablespoons ghee

2 tablespoons liquid glucose

No baking required here – just a block of sweetened, thickened, granular milk carved into squares – simply satisfying!

IMARTI

INGREDIENTS

⅓ cup skinless split black gram

1 tablespoon cornflour

A few drops of orange food colour

1 cup (250 grams) sugar

Ghee for deep-frying

Known as jangri in the south, this popular variant of jalebi has thicker, juicier coils in a distinctive design.

METHOD

Soak the split black gram for about two to three hours. Drain and grind with the cornflour, food colour and one-fourth cup plus one tablespoon of water to a fine batter. The batter should have the consistency of cake batter.

In a non-stick pan, cook the sugar with one cup of water, stirring till the sugar dissolves. Add the milk and collect the scum, which rises to the surface with a ladle, and discard. Cook till the mixture attains a one-string consistency (see note on page 7). Remove from heat and keep the syrup warm. Heat sufficient ghee in a shallow non-stick pan.

Pour the batter into a squeeze bottle. Pipe out the batter into the hot ghee in two concentric circles in a clockwise direction, followed by scallops in an anti-clockwise direction. Deep-fry till golden on both sides.

Remove with a slotted spoon and soak in the warm sugar syrup for fifteen minutes. Drain and serve hot.

- Makes 500 grams

PINNI

METHOD

Soak the split black gram for at least one hour in three cups of water. Drain and grind to a fine paste, with seven tablespoons of water.

Heat the ghee in a deep non-stick pan. Add the semolina, gram flour and flour, and sauté for five minutes. Add the ground *dal* and continue to sauté on low heat for about half an hour.

Cook the sugar and half a cup of water, stirring till the sugar dissolves. Add the milk, collect the scum, which rises to the surface with a ladle, and discard. Cook to make a syrup of one-string consistency (see note on page 7).

Add the *khoya* to the black gram mixture and cook for five minutes. Add the cardamom powder and mix.

Stir in the sugar syrup and cook for a while longer till the mixture dries up a little. Add the almonds, take the pan off the heat and leave to cool.

Divide the cold mixture into twelve to sixteen equal portions and shape each portion into a round or oval *pinni*.

■ Makes 12-16 *pinni*

INGREDIENTS

1¼ cups skinless split black gram

¾ cup (160 grams) pure ghee

2½ tablespoons semolina

1½ tablespoons gram flour

½ tablespoon wholewheat flour

1 cup (250 grams) sugar

2 teaspoons milk

3 tablespoons almond slivers, roasted

¾ cup (135 grams) *khoya/mawa*, grated

½ teaspoon green cardamom powder

Nostalgia and a trip down memory lane – *pinni* has that effect on me. I am transported back to my childhood in Punjab, when simple pleasures came in sweet balls of dough.

MOHANTHAAL

INGREDIENTS

2 cups (200 grams) coarse gram flour

¾ cup + 1½ tablespoons (180 grams) ghee

3 tablespoons milk

1½ cups (375 grams) sugar

2 teaspoons milk

5-6 saffron threads

¼ teaspoon green cardamom powder

A large pinch of nutmeg powder

10 almonds, blanched and slivered

10 pistachios, blanched and slivered

My mother-in-law makes the most awesome Mohanthaal, a traditional Gujarati *mithai*. It is one of those versatile soul-satisfying sweets that fulfil several needs – a comfort food, a pick-me-up, or a celebratory offering.

METHOD

Place the gram flour in a bowl. Heat a non-stick pan; add one and a half tablespoons ghee and two tablespoons milk and warm slightly. Add this to the gram flour and mix with your fingertips till the mixture resembles breadcrumbs. Pass through a thick sieve so that the crumbs are smooth.

Grease an eight-inch *thali*.

Heat the remaining ghee in a thick-bottomed non-stick pan. Add the gram flour mixture and cook on medium heat till fragrant and darker in colour.

Meanwhile, cook the sugar and half a cup of water, stirring till the sugar dissolves. Add two teaspoons milk and collect the scum, which rises to the surface with a ladle, and discard. Cook to make a syrup of one-and-a-half string consistency (see note on page 7).

Soak the saffron in one tablespoon of warm milk for ten minutes. Add it to sugar syrup and mix well.

Add half the cardamom powder and nutmeg powder to the gram flour and mix. Take the pan off the heat and keep stirring till the mixture cools completely.

Add the syrup to the gram flour mixture and stir continuously, till all the liquid is absorbed and the mixture thickens and becomes a little dry.

Pour the mixture into the greased *thali* and spread evenly. Smooth the top and sprinkle the almonds and pistachios. Sprinkle the remaining cardamom powder and set aside to cool. Cut into squares and serve.

■ Makes 500 grams

Chef's Tip: If the gram flour mixture dries up while cooking, sprinkle a little milk.

MYSORE PAAK

METHOD

Dry-roast the gram flour in a thick-bottomed non-stick pan on medium heat till light brown and fragrant.

Melt the ghee in another non-stick pan and simmer over low heat. Grease a six-by-eight-inch aluminium tray with a little ghee.

Cook the sugar with one cup of water and the milk, stirring till the sugar dissolves. Collect the scum, which rises to the surface with a ladle, and discard. Cook till the syrup attains a one-string consistency (see note on page 7).

Add the gram flour, a little by little and cook, stirring continuously. Add the hot ghee, a little by little and mix well. Every time you add the ghee, the mixture should sizzle and froth.

Continue to cook, stirring, till all the ghee has been used up, and the mixture thickens and leaves the sides of the pan. Quickly transfer the mixture onto the greased tray and spread evenly and smooth the surface.

Cool a little and cut into squares. Separate the squares when completely cold and store in an air-tight container.

- Makes 750 grams

INGREDIENTS

1 cup (100 grams) gram flour

2 cups (500 grams) sugar

2 teaspoons milk

1⅔ cups (355 grams) pure ghee

Believed to have been created in the kitchens of the Mysore palace, this sumptuous, honeycombed *mithai* saturated with the purest ghee lives up to its royal beginnings.

GLOSSARY

English	Hindi	English	Hindi
Almonds	Badam	Jaggery	Gur
Alum	Phitkari	Mango, ripe	Aam
Ash gourd	Petha	Milk	Doodh
Banana	Kela	Nutmeg	Jaiphal
Black gram, skinless split	Dhuli urad dal	Peanuts	Moongphalli
Butter	Makkhan	Pistachios	Pista
Carrots	Gajar	Pointed gourd	Parwal
Cashew Nut	Kaju	Pomegranate kernels	Anardana
Caster sugar	Pisihui shakkar	Poppy seeds	Khuskhus
Cloves	Laung	Puffed rice	Kurmura
Cream	Malai	Raisins	Kishmish
Dates	Khajur	Refined flour	Maida
Desiccated coconut	Namirahit khopra ka bareek choora	Roasted Bengal gram	Daalia
		Saffron	Kesar
Edible gum resin	Gond	Screw pine	Kewda
Edible silver foil	Chandi ka varq	Semolina	Sooji/rawa
Fennel	Badi saunf	Sesame seeds	Til
Figs, dried	Anjeer	Slate lime powder	Chuna
Fresh coconut	Nariyal	Vinegar	Sirka
Gram flour	Besan	Walnuts	Akhrot
Green cardamom	Chhoti elaichi	Wholewheat flour	Atta
Guava	Amrud	Yogurt	Dahi

Sanjeev Kapoor

Mithai

www.popularprakashan.com